Family Mediation

Robert Coulson

Family Mediation

Managing Conflict, Resolving Disputes

Second Edition

Jossey-Bass Publishers • San Francisco

First edition of *Family Mediation* published in 1994 by the American Arbitration Association. Originally published as *Fighting Fair* in 1983 by The Free Press.

Substantial discounts on bulk quantities of Jossey-Bass books are available to corporations, professional associations, and other organizations. For details and discount information, contact the special sales department at Jossey-Bass Inc., Publishers (415) 433–1740; Fax (800) 605–2665.

For sales outside the United States, please contact your local Simon & Schuster International office.

 Manufactured in the United States of America on Lyons Falls Pathfinder Tradebook. This paper is acid-free and 100 percent totally chlorine-free.

Library of Congress Cataloging-in-Publication Data

Coulson, Robert, date.
    Family mediation : managing conflict, resolving disputes / Robert Coulson. — 2nd ed.
      p. cm.
    Includes bibliographical references and index.
    ISBN 0-7879-0312-4 (cloth : acid-free paper)
    1. Family mediation—United States.   2. Divorce mediation—United States.   3. Dispute resolution (Law)—United States.
4. Domestic relations—United States.   I. Title.
KF505.C68   1996
362.82'86—dc20   96-25262

FIRST EDITION
HB Printing   10 9 8 7 6 5 4 3 2 1

Contents

Preface

Family disputes are better settled privately than in court, and competent mediators can often help. This book is about the techniques and the services of family mediators, and about how you can become one.

As president of the American Arbitration Association for more than twenty years, I administered systems that every year handled tens of thousands of cases on many kinds of issues through arbitration and mediation. The experience confirmed my belief that people should be encouraged to use arbitration and mediation to resolve their disagreements. A lawsuit is the worst way to settle a controversy; those who go to court are often victimized by the process of litigation.

Many kinds of family disputes, some of them described here, can be mediated. Even if you don't become a family mediator, I encourage you to think like one, because it will help you resolve disagreements in your own life. Mediation is an art and a vocational skill, but it also provides positive strategies for managing conflict. In that sense, this book is for everyone who becomes involved in family problems.

A surge of interest in private dispute resolution—later called alternative dispute resolution or ADR—came in the late 1960s. One reason was that many people were deciding that they did not want to give control of their disputes to attorneys; community mediation was a direct result. Another reason was a backlog in the courts, which made it difficult for judges to give prompt attention to cases; various ADR systems were devised to deal with that problem. Also, the business community had become concerned about the costs and delays of litigation, creating a demand for new and efficient dispute resolution mechanisms. Corporate lawyers and academics were therefore encouraged to study mediation and other forms of private dispute resolution and see if they could be applied to various business situations.

Family mediation was one result of all these trends. It was based on the belief that families should be encouraged to settle their own disputes and the knowledge that family courts were overburdened. Some experts wondered whether divorce negotiations and other family controversies could be settled through mediation, rather than through bargaining by divorce lawyers on the courthouse steps. Many families seemed to be in court because they didn't know where else to go.

In the early 1970s the American Arbitration Association called a meeting of social workers, family therapists, divorce lawyers, and a few family mediators, including Sheila Kessler, Mark Lohman, and the late O. J. Coogler. The purpose of the meeting was to discuss whether private mediation could be used to settle family disputes before they ripened into lawsuits. The response was positive.

Social workers recognized that mediation could fundamentally change how families are helped. Encouraging clients to resolve their own disputes was an attractive idea. One executive director of a family service agency put it this way: "If mediation works, I can see our agency giving it a high priority. We believe that a trained mediator can help people manage their own problems. If we can teach our clients to settle their disputes on their own, they will be better off. Any time you can keep someone out of court, they are likely to be better off."

Some participants saw mediation as a service they could offer to their clients. Family therapists were particularly intrigued. Many therapists considered litigation destructive, whereas mediation had the potential of strengthening the family. As one psychologist explained: "The way the agreement is reached can be equally important as the agreement itself. If the process allows the parties to participate, they may be more likely to believe that any settlement that results is fair."

In general, the participants supported the notion that parties should be encouraged to use mediation. This meeting contributed to the momentum of the family mediation movement.

After the meeting, I was asked to see what could be done to develop the practice of family mediation. During the next several years, the American Arbitration Association drafted family mediation rules, provided basic training for family mediators, and publicized the availability of the service. My book *Fighting Fair: Family Mediation Will Work for You* was published by The Free Press in 1983, and I made many presentations on the subject to community organizations and on television and radio. Other people began to do the same. Soon it became clear that family mediation would be marketed on a local basis; mediators would have to develop their own practice. Training would be carried out by specialized organizations, many of them created by individual mediators. The American Arbitration Association gradually reduced its family mediation activities, recognizing that the field would develop in those ways.

I continued my interest in the field not because I had aspirations of becoming a family mediator, but because family mediation had the capacity for providing a rational, accessible and humane service. At first I saw the role of the mediator as limited to helping parties bargain, much as union and management do in labor relations, but I gradually realized that the function was more complex, involving collaboration, enhanced communications, behavioral modification, and family therapy, in addition to traditional negotiating skills. I also became aware of the need for lawyers and other professionals to make this powerful dispute management tool part of their practice.

When I first spoke about divorce mediation—in 1974 at the annual meeting of the Family Law Section of the American Bar Association in Atlanta, Georgia—family mediation was relatively new and likely to be rejected by divorce lawyers. Several of them in the audience that day were sharply critical. They said that mediation would never work. It was essential, they told me, for each spouse to be represented by a divorce lawyer. I wondered about that then, and in the intervening years I have concluded that they were reflecting professional bias.

By now the picture has changed. Lawyers routinely refer clients to mediation. Some, especially among members of the Family Law Section, serve as family mediators themselves. The American Bar Association has even formed a Section on Dispute Resolution to encourage the use of mediation and other forms of alternative dispute resolution; I served as a member of the council of that section. Bar associations all over the world now encourage family mediation. The question today is not whether lawyers will participate in the process, but whether they may attempt to dominate it.

Practicing family mediators are available in many communities, but there is room for more. I want to encourage qualified people to become family mediators, which is why I wrote this book: it answers many commonly asked questions about family mediation. Still, the best way to learn how to mediate is to do it on a regular basis. Experience leads to a more positive attitude and to a concentration on problem solving rather than confrontation. You learn to listen carefully, to understand other people's needs and aspirations. Mediation not only encourages responsible behavior, but offers a practical way to manage conflict and resolve disputes.

Family mediators have created a professional organization of their own, the Academy of Family Mediators, which provides a full range of services to its members. I refer to the academy many times in this book because it can be a helpful resource for anyone who wants to know more about family mediation. The Academy of Family Mediators can be reached at 4 Militia Drive, Lexington, Mass., 02173. The fax number is (617) 674–2690.

Another useful resource is the Society of Professionals in Dispute Resolution (SPIDR), less focused on family issues than the academy but interested in all forms of ADR. SPIDR can be contacted at 815 15th Street, Washington, D.C., 20005. The fax number is (202) 783–7281.

The American Arbitration Association has generously allowed me to use some of the material that originally appeared in *Fighting Fair*, but this book is written from a different point of view and with a deeper understanding of the process.

I would like to thank Susan Klein, head of the publication department of the American Arbitration Association, for encouraging me to write another book on family mediation. Thanks to Sue also for her friendship and assistance over many years.

Riverside, Connecticut   Robert Coulson
July 1996

The Author

Robert Coulson served as president of the American Arbitration Association (AAA) for over twenty years. He retired in 1994 after working there since 1963. Coulson has written and lectured all over the world on dispute resolution. Among his prior publications are *How to Stay Out of Court* (1968), which popularized alternative dispute resolution, *Business Mediation* (1987), and *Fighting Fair* (1983), an early book on family mediation.

A graduate of Yale University and Harvard Law School, Coulson received the William Nelson Cromwell Award from the New York County Lawyers in 1993 and honorary doctorates from Hofstra University and Bryant College. For many years he served on the board of the Federation of Protestant Welfare Agencies of New York. In addition, he has headed dispute resolution committees of the American Bar Association, the Association of the Bar of the City of New York, and the Society of Professionals in Dispute Resolution, of which he was a founding member. He is also a member of the Academy of Family Mediators.

Coulson lives in Connecticut with his wife of thirty-six years, Cynthia, a magazine editor.

Family Mediation

Chapter One

The Nature of Family Disputes

The family is America's primary social institution, but dramatic changes have taken place in its structure. Some are obvious: for example, the average family size has declined for several generations and in 1994 stood at 2.67 people per family (*Information Please Almanac*, 1996, p. 747). This has been caused by falling birth rates, a higher percentage of working women, a more mobile and self-indulgent lifestyle, and increasingly permissive divorce laws, among other reasons.

Many Americans live alone. Some are elderly, but many are young and yet to marry, or formerly married and separated. One of every three births is to an unmarried mother, and the percentage continues to climb (*Information Please Almanac*, 1996, p. 838). Fewer couples are marrying, particularly those with relatively low levels of education and income. Obviously, education and income are related factors; it has become difficult for someone without at least a high school education to earn enough money to marry. Some government policies such as welfare benefits for single mothers and various income tax provisions applicable to middle- and upper-income taxpayers actually encourage the trend by making it less attractive to marry and penalizing those who do.

Different lifestyles are evolving, including unmarried couples, single-parent families, binuclear families, couples without children, same-sex couples, and unrelated groups living together with or without children. These various nontraditional families involve people who share many of the obligations and advantages of traditional family life. When adults pool their resources, their bonds are

1

like those that keep nuclear families together, combining compatibility with other practical considerations. Like nuclear families, these groupings generate interpersonal disputes that must be resolved; thus this book treats them as families.

The traditional family still exists, with children and an at-home mother supported by a working father, but increasing numbers of women have acquired economic independence through employment. Some have achieved earning equality with their husbands. Aside from income generation, other traditional family roles also have been in transition, and general equality between husband and wife is now much more common than in the past.

But change creates stress. Each year, over a million American families break up; half of all marriages end in divorce, leaving millions of children in single-parent homes (*Information Please Almanac*, 1996, p. 823). Nuclear families become binuclear or multinuclear. Sometimes the relationship between a child and an absent parent is completely lost, but most children retain some sort of relationship with their absent parents and with the other adults who share their lives.

The United States is not homogeneous when it comes to income and family structure, but rather like a patchwork quilt. Income levels have diverged in recent years. For the poorest of the poor, the family structure has become threadbare. In some disadvantaged neighborhoods, fewer than one out of five children live with their natural fathers. This is a global trend; America has the world's highest percentage of one-parent households, but Australia, Britain, Canada, and the Scandinavian countries are close behind (*Information Please Almanac*, 1996, p. 432). Fractured families are present at every income level, but the social profile of an inner-city housing project is quite different from that of an upscale suburb, and family mediators have to use different tactics in different communities.

It is misleading to generalize about the American family. Politicians are typically fond of doing so during their runs for office, but much of what they say is wishful thinking and is not often reflected in the policies they pursue. They proclaim a dedication to family values, but social programs for children in need are much less comprehensive in the United States than in Europe. The American Way seems to favor national priorities geared to the needs of adults; whatever the politics behind this, it highlights the problems many families face in a free-enterprise society, the pressures that create stress and lead to disputes.

A common issue in family courts is determining whether a parent is capable of and willing to take responsibility for nurturing a child. The increased number of low-income unmarried mothers is one reason. Of mothers on welfare in 1993, 55 percent were not married (*Information Please Almanac*, 1996, p. 836) and courts are obliged to intervene when they become incapable of caring for their children.

When parents decide to live apart, child care often becomes a matter for negotiations between the parents. The most intractable issues are usually custody, visitation, and financial support, which the courts are not well suited to resolve because they do not have enough time to listen to the parents. In most cases it would be better for everyone if those arrangements could be made by the family and in private. Voluntary mediation makes that possible.

Who Can Use Family Mediation?

Family controversies come wrapped in an almost impenetrable gauze of past relationships. A mediator can help the parties unwrap those bundles and determine why they are at odds and how to resolve the controversy. Mediation is no panacea, but it encourages a realistic approach to problems and provides an opportunity to settle disputes equitably, reasonably, and directly. That is an idyllic view of the process; it also was called a "value-laden, surreptitiously quasi-coercive process, in which parties are led or manipulated into redesigning their perceptions so that they can arrive at a common definition of the problem and its solution" in an article by Alan C. Tidwell (1994, pp. 3, 4), more about which later.

Family mediation is a process by which a neutral mediator assists family members in resolving their disputes. Often it is undertaken by married couples who need help working out the terms of a separation agreement leading to divorce: child custody, property division, and the like. Private family mediators can help with many other disputes as well, including premarital agreements, gay partnerships, quarrels between teenagers and their parents, disputes over a family business, and other disagreements within families. The definition above refers to private, volunteer family mediation. Another form of mediation has been established by state law in more than thirty states on a mandatory or discretionary basis to resolve custody disputes (Gaschen, 1995, pp. 473–474). By whatever definition, family mediation has demonstrated a remarkable ability to bring couples together to the point of settlement. It works. There is a market for it.

Family mediation has six basic principles: party determination, informed consent, confidentiality, good faith negotiation, competent and impartial mediators, and concern for the interests of children and others. Party determination means that the people whose dispute is at issue make most of the procedural decisions and all of the substantive decisions in reaching a mutually agreeable settlement. Informed consent means that after they are told by the mediator exactly how the mediation process works, they both agree to participate and to negotiate in good faith. The process is confidential in that the mediator will never disclose what is said in a session to anyone else. The mediator should bring sufficient experience and knowledge to the process and show no preference to either party. Furthermore, the mediator must encourage both parties to devote sufficient attention and concern to the interests of their children and other interested third parties.

These principles are essential and interactive, though they sometimes conflict with each other as well. For example, a mediator usually would feel it mandatory to encourage a woman to exercise self-determination in a conflict with her husband, but could not reasonably do so if the husband will physically abuse her when she stands up to him.

For this and other reasons, mediation is not for everyone. Some people can work out the terms of their separation without any outside assistance, while others need legal or psychological support; some may have to be forced by court order to accept family obligations; some may simply be unwilling or incapable of bargaining in good faith. But most people are willing to negotiate and know that reaching agreement is better than being dragged into court. Litigation, after all, is usually unpleasant and expensive; both parties have to give up control, hire lawyers, and submit to a judge. When opposing lawyers are injected into a family dispute, they may create additional controversies. Bitterness and hostility may ripen into all-consuming litigation that is even more disruptive and costly. The final result, whether fashioned by a judge or hammered out by lawyers before reaching the courtroom, may be unsatisfactory to both parties; at any rate it likely will have been gained only after a chaotic and destructive battle that exposes the spiteful aspects of their characters.

Mediation, on the other hand, gives the parties control over their dispute. They can sit down, solve problems, and cling to whatever remains of their mutual respect.

It is healthy for a family to bicker. A conflict-free environment may be undesirable even in the unlikely event that it is attainable. Arguments provide an opportunity for family members to engage in the give-and-take of living together, which encourages growth and leads to individual development. Quarrels can be stimulating. They are particularly important for adolescents, who need to test their adversarial skills. For them, negotiating provides a key to the adult world.

Not every disagreement has to be resolved. Parents learn to expect flurries of confrontational behavior from adolescents. These are regarded as normal events on the way to maturity and may not require serious negotiations, but families should feel free to argue in a positive way. In more serious conflicts, however, they may benefit from a mediated negotiation that brings out the healthy aspects of dispute resolution and helps squelch the kind of squabbling that can be destructive and spiteful.

Many people respond to controversy by attempting to fix blame, which is often a waste of time; better to identify the problem, which allows it to be dealt with. In any case, fixing blame is never easy. In all likelihood the person who seemed at fault was provoked. Someone may have pushed the situation beyond the point of reconciliation. Mediators may have to persuade their clients to analyze why the provocation took place. Was it intentional? Did either party intend to create the disagreement? Mediators ask questions but do not answer them; their job is to help clients find the answers themselves by bringing out the facts and encouraging each party's self-determination.

Mediation encourages people to manage their own disputes. It can also provide a powerful learning experience. With the help of a mediator, those who disagree can create a working relationship that makes it possible to settle their differences.

Parties to mediation authorize an impartial person to help them negotiate a consensual and informed settlement. Equally important, however, are the therapeutic and educational functions of family mediation that allow people to gain important insights about themselves and enhance their understanding of how future disagreements can be resolved. A family mediator not only helps settle the current dispute, but encourages a more realistic view of the future. Relationships within the family can be strengthened not by smarmy attempts to get the parties to love each other but by persuading them to collaborate. A mediator encourages clients to settle not because they like each other but because the agreed-upon solution will work—because it makes sense. They are free to retain their differences in values or perspectives; about those, they can continue to disagree.

Decision-making authority rests with the parties. A mediator does not tell them how to settle, but may warn how difficult their lives may become if they are unable to resolve the dispute. A mediator encourages negotiation in good faith and entrance into a mutually acceptable and enforceable settlement. This is done by reducing the obstacles to communication, maximizing the exploration of alternatives, and addressing the needs of those involved or affected.

The family mediator's services cannot be described simply; they involve working through the clients and considering all the complexities and antagonisms of their relationship and the contrasting perceptions they bring to the negotiations. Moreover, the mediator's relationship with the clients changes during the process. At first, one or both parties may seek the mediator's support for their positions, intending to use that support in their negotiations and calculating how to gain the advantage. They try to figure out how to manipulate the mediator to obtain the best possible result in the negotiations. Neither is interested in fine ideals; they both want to win.

Practical Matters: Who Mediates and What It Costs

Family mediators have various backgrounds, work for various organizations or for themselves, and use various mediation techniques. These factors influence who uses family mediation and under what circumstances it is used, as well as what types of people decide to become mediators themselves.

Types of Family Mediators

Some mediators are mental health professionals such as social workers, psychologists, or family counselors. Many mental health professionals work in public mediation programs sponsored by the courts. Of the family mediators who are in private practice, an increasing percentage are lawyers. Some mediators work at it part-time and have a different primary avocation. Perhaps because family mediation is interdisciplinary, no one profession dominates the practice.

Mediators bring particular kinds of knowledge and ability to their work. The profession requires a combination of expertise not usually found in any other single field, a range that crosses many boundaries but includes general knowledge of conflict resolution, domestic relations law and other laws that affect families, family organization, and various helping skills such as communications, case management, and interviewing. In addition, mediators must be able to work with other professionals who help families cope with their problems.

Family mediators are available throughout the United States. Many are members of the Academy of Family Mediators, an association that serves their interests. To any potential client, the academy will supply the names of practitioners, including academy members and others, who meet its criteria (these criteria are listed in Chapter Five). Many well-qualified people practice family mediation without the academy's "practitioner" designation, but those who have it demonstrate at least a minimum degree of training and experience.

Some family mediators are listed in the Yellow Pages. According to academy guidelines, mediators may advertise their services as long as the information in their ads is accurate. The academy also encourages family mediators to promote mediation by participating in educational programs. Many mediators appear on radio or television or give lectures on family-related subjects, through which they become known in their communities.

To determine competence and the use of methods consistent with their needs, the parties to a mediation usually schedule a joint interview with their prospective mediator. They should ask questions about the mediator's background, training, and experience as a family mediator, and then find out what procedures the mediator follows and how many sessions are likely to be necessary to solve their problems.

At any such advance interview, a mediator should provide accurate information about all the above, and should also divulge any strong personal or professional views about whatever issues are likely to be involved in the mediation. If the prospective clients ask for references, as they normally ought to, the mediator should provide the names of former clients who have given their consent.

Mediation procedures vary considerably. Some mediators use family therapy. Others stress communications. Still others involve clients in training programs on parenting. One party in a prospective mediation may prefer a particular mediator's approach while the other party prefers another. But it is imperative that the mediator be acceptable to both parties.

A delicate relationship is created between the mediator and the parties, so clients should feel comfortable with the mediator they select; each should have confidence in that person's ability and independence.

Paying for Family Mediation

Some family mediators offer their services for a fee. Others are employed by nonprofit organizations. Some are retained by family courts. Still others volunteer to help their friends or family or community group.

Most independent professional family mediators expect to be paid for their services and usually charge by the hour at a rate agreed upon when the parties meet with the mediator for the first time. At that meeting, all fees and related costs should be explained, their allocation between the parties decided, and the time and method of payment spelled out. This should be incorporated in a written retainer agreement that both clients sign. Some part of the fee may be payable in advance.

Any party who thinks a mediator's fees are too high can refuse to go forward and make no further commitment. The hourly fee may be negotiable, but clients should bear in mind that mediation can be time-consuming. Reaching agreements on some issues in advance and coming to the mediation prepared to make additional concessions, if possible, will expedite final settlement and reduce the cost.

According to the Academy of Family Mediators, fees must be "fair, reasonable and commensurate with the service to be performed" (Academy of Family Mediators Standards of Practice,

IV[B], 1995). They should be spelled out in advance. It is inappropriate for mediators to charge contingent fees or to base fees on the outcome of mediation, nor should they pay commissions, give rebates, or make similar payments for referrals. Also, clients should be permitted to withdraw from mediation at any time, paying only for the time already spent.

Services provided by community mediation centers may be free or available for only a nominal fee. Often these centers use volunteer mediators, sometimes private practitioners serving their communities in their spare time. Most such centers serve low-income clients whose cases nevertheless may be complex. In one case, for example, a woman sought a temporary restraining order against her estranged husband, who had been making abusive telephone calls to her. He ran a small business, she worked part-time driving a school bus, and they had three small children and very little money. Their case was assigned to a community mediation service, where the mediator learned that the couple had a long history of fighting and had been separated once before. Soon the mediator discovered that most of their problems revolved around the wife's demands for money and the couple's basic inability to cope. Resolution was arrived at by scheduling specific times for the husband's phone calls (with an understanding that his phone would be disconnected if he violated the agreement), and a separation agreement that obliged the husband to make modest support payments. The couple lived for a year under this agreement, then reunited.

Sometimes courts mandate mediation, as in California where child custody issues are required by law to be mediated (Gaschen, 1995); in such cases, the costs are usually paid by the state. In some statutory, court-based mediations, one or both parties are ordered to pay for it. A few civil courts mandate the payment of lawyer mediators, which can be expensive.

The least costly mediation is the informal kind within a family or community. Those who help friends or families resolve disputes are mediators whether they know it or not, and the techniques used by professionals can work just as well for amateurs. For that matter, mediation can be internalized; families can approach disputes as if they were working with a professional mediator, seeking amicable solutions and adopting reasonable positions in order to reach a settlement.

The Mediation Process

Private mediators serve at the pleasure of their clients, who are there voluntarily. The Academy of Family Mediators says that the parties should have the right to withdraw at any time and for any reason, or for no reason.

The negotiations also belong to the clients. If they settle, fine. If they do not, they can try to end their dispute without a mediator, or hire a new one. They can arbitrate, go to court, or, if it comes to that, they can flip a coin and let God be their adjudicator.

A mediator can also withdraw, deciding, for example, that the parties are not serious about wanting to settle their dispute. The Academy of Family Mediators puts it this way: "If the mediator believes that the participants are unable or unwilling to participate meaningfully in the process or that a reasonable agreement is unlikely, the mediator may suspend or terminate mediation and should encourage the parties to seek professional help" (Academy of Family Mediators Standards of Practice, IX[D], 1995).

Thus the mediator can withdraw, but this language seems to place the onus on the clients, which raises some interesting questions. Can a mediator quit without giving any reason? Can a mediator withdraw because the parties are meeting without the mediator, or making agreements the mediator thinks are improper? What is a "reasonable" agreement? Is it the duty of the mediator to determine whether the settlement is reasonable?

These questions will be addressed in depth later, but certainly the possibility of the mediator withdrawing for whatever reason can encourage parties to negotiate in good faith. On the other hand, it may give one party an opportunity to frustrate the negotiations without having to declare an impasse; this is one example of the tactical moves some parties make in mediation. Not every party wants the mediation to end in a settlement. The mediator is expendable. One or both parties may be using mediation to buy time or obtain information without any intention of reaching settlement; they want the mediation to fail.

Private family mediation only comes into play when the parties agree to make use of it. Most family disputes are resolved informally, without mediators or any other outsiders. Families work out their problems by themselves. They only need help when there is a crisis, such as an impending divorce, a fight for control of a family business, or some other problem that requires substantial concessions. At that point an experienced mediator can be helpful, but only if the parties are willing to negotiate. If they can't even talk to each other, mediation may be impossible. But that is unusual; most people are willing to discuss their disagreements, particularly if they see some possibility of a settlement. They don't want to destroy their relationships with other members of the family.

Two Typical Divorce Mediations

The desire to maintain family continuity may not seem so obvious when a couple are getting a divorce. They may be angry and quite prepared to fight, but even then most people realize that they will have to accept certain mutual obligations, particularly when children are involved. Someone must provide parental care. Someone will have to cover family expenses.

A few divorcing couples will decide on their own to use a mediator, but more typically they are referred to mediation, perhaps by an attorney. Whether the lawyer is a friend to the couple or their legal adviser, it is increasingly common to recommend family mediation to try to reach an amicable settlement. Consider two typical cases.

Bill and Jane.   After three years of marriage, living in the same house and sharing expenses, Bill and Jane were unhappy. It was a first marriage for both; they had no children and good incomes, $60,000 a year for Bill and $45,000 for Jane. After talking with a marriage counselor, they concluded that they were incompatible and decided to seek a divorce, but they wanted to be fair to each other. The therapist suggested using a mediator, and recommended an attorney specializing in domestic relations law who had developed a separate family mediation practice.

Bill and Jane accepted the recommendation. At a preliminary meeting, the mediator explained how she worked and Bill and Jane decided to go forward, signing a retainer agreement. As the mediator knew nothing about their situation, they explained it to her. Every case is unique, but the mediator had a general knowledge of the issues that were likely to be relevant, and in this case nothing seemed too unusual. She asked questions, which helped identify points that needed to be negotiated.

But then Jane began to blame Bill for the failure of the marriage. Soon the couple was involved in a heated argument. The mediator allowed it to continue until Jane began to cry, and then suspended the meeting, telling her clients to come back with additional financial information.

At the next session, the mediator began by encouraging Bill and Jane to concentrate on the remaining items in dispute. They came to terms fairly quickly on several items, planned to meet later to discuss dividing their furniture, and on a few issues agreed to develop proposals that could be discussed at the next session. The major sticking point appeared to be who would remain in the house.

The mediator had expected to reach final agreement at the third session, but the mood changed. Bill and Jane's meeting about the furniture had turned into an argument, and now they were angry and unable to agree. So the mediator listed all the contested possessions on a display board, and Bill and Jane took turns selecting items on the list. They still couldn't agree on a few; to the mediator it seemed that those represented the finality of ending their relationship. She talked to them about it, asking them how to resolve the problem. After considering what she had said, Bill and Jane conceded that none of the items had tangible value and finally divided them up. Before sending them away, the mediator suggested that they think about their joint interest in their home, which was to be the subject of the next session, and perhaps discuss it with an attorney.

The final session was relatively calm. By then, Bill and Jane were comfortable with the process; they decided to sell their house and share the proceeds equally. At the end, the mediator gave them a memorandum reflecting their understanding. Another attorney would draft a formal separation agreement to be filed in court with their divorce petition.

This was a successful mediation. After their initial squabble, Bill and Jane were able to negotiate in good faith. The mediator helped them reach a settlement, and the outcome was satisfactory to both parties.

Is that typical? Between 60 percent and 80 percent of divorce mediations result in settlement (Kelly, 1993, p. 138). For example, in one experimental program, 77 percent of custody cases randomly assigned to mediation by a court settled, compared to 31 percent of those assigned to lawyer negotiations (Kelly, 1993, p. 151).

Parties who agree to meet with a mediator may be predisposed to reach agreement, but they nevertheless need help to get there. The competence of the mediator may contribute to an even higher success rate; there seems no reason why mediators should not be judged, at least in part, on their percentage of settlements.

Alex and Pat.   When children are involved, divorce mediation may be more complicated. After ten years of marriage and a separation of less than a year, Alex was living with another woman and a jealous Pat had filed for divorce. Alex demanded custody of their two daughters, and the lawyers were licking their chops as they geared up to try the case in divorce court.

But one day Alex had a discussion with one of his colleagues at work. "You must be nuts, Alex," said the friend. "Do you know how much that divorce is going to cost you?" Alex replied that he couldn't give up his kids, but the friend responded: "Let me ask you, do you love your kids? Sure you do. Why don't you sit down with Pat and a family mediator and talk about what's best for the children? You're too smart to waste money on lawyers. Get with it."

One of Pat's friends gave her the same message. At any rate, Alex and Pat agreed to mediate. Early in the first session they fought with each other, but the mediator soon realized that much of Pat's anger came from jealousy. Privately, she pointed out to Pat that it was time to forget those feelings and get on with her life. After that, Alex and Pat were able to discuss their mutual problems.

They still argued about custody. The mediator discovered they didn't understand what legal custody meant, so she assigned each of them an article to read; by the second session, they could discuss the subject in a more informed way. Both were concerned for their children, so she reminded them what would be involved in bringing up two little girls; later they agreed on joint custody in which the children would live with Pat but Alex would have liberal access rights to them and would have a say in how they were brought up. After five sessions, Pat and Alex were able to resolve all of their disagreements. And by then, Pat was beginning to date again and Alex was engaged.

Jessica Pearson, a leading researcher in the field and the person who supplied the Pat-and-Alex example, believes that mediation is often less expensive, faster, and more satisfactory to both parties than litigation. Her studies indicate that those who reach agreements through mediation may be less likely to go to court, at least during the early years of their agreement (Pearson and Thoennes, 1989). Other research, as will be mentioned later, concurs.

In a healthy family, negotiations are ongoing and its members trade concessions every day. The process is so automatic that they may not realize what is going on. They may never need mediation because they expect to have disagreements, know how to manage them, and know how to resolve them. Some couples can even decide to separate amicably, but may need help to resolve such emotional issues as child custody, which they may encounter only once in their lives. Mediators deal with such issues often, however, and know how they are likely to be resolved. Experience helps; a competent family mediator can guide people through negotiations while avoiding sources of disagreement.

One divorce mediator puts it this way: "Clients don't come to me because they enjoy my company. They have heard how expensive it can be to negotiate through lawyers. They may have tried it themselves. If they couldn't agree on their own and needed some help, someone sent them to me."

Mediation is an attractive alternative when the issues are complicated or involve strong feelings, or when the parties are having difficulty dealing with each other; an experienced family mediator can help bring about settlement. It does not always do the trick, but mediation leaves decision-making power where it belongs—in the hands of the parties concerned—and usually leads to realistic settlement. For most family disputes, mediation is much better than going to court.

Mediation focuses on the needs, wants, and concerns of each party, as well as the lives they will lead after a settlement is reached. It is an efficient and practical way to negotiate. Mediation combines bargaining and collaboration; the parties may come to it with divergent views but often alter their perceptions as they become committed to the process and then converge into settlement.

The breakup of a marriage illustrates this. In divorce, the parties must abandon the empty shell of marriage and set forth upon a new, independent life. They may find it difficult to imagine their lives after divorce, basing their expectations on illusion. But both must learn how to live without a spouse, and if they have children, both must still provide for their care. All of this requires readjustments that are not easy to make without knowing exactly what problems need to be resolved and without clearly understanding the needs and concerns of the spouse. Such uncertainties, topped off with inevitable feelings of rejection and misery, can add up to an explosive combination of anxiety, anger, and ignorance.

An important function of the divorce mediator is to help clients cope with the resentment that often surfaces when marital relationships are in shreds and that can destroy whatever remains of their love and mutual admiration. A mediator will try to salvage what was positive in their relationship, not with the expectation that they will reunite but to provide the foundation for an agreement, so that when the marriage contract ends, it can be replaced by a newly created partnership based on trust and respect rather than love. Family relationships are not being eliminated, merely restructured.

The terms and conditions of the agreement are important, but equally so is an exploration of the parties' attitudes toward each other and their children. Mediation gives them a chance to talk about their remaining obligations to family relationships; with the mediator as a guide, they may come to a better understanding of such responsibilities. The parental aspects of divorce call out for collaboration, which is why some mediators place them first on their agenda.

Two Schools of Mediation

Some family mediators believe that mediation can foster behavioral modification. That approach has been called the therapeutic school.

The Therapeutic School.   Mediators who follow this school attempt to help the parties cope with whatever psychological problems seem to be blocking effective problem-solving, usually intervening when a blockage is identified.

These mediators are often mental health professionals. They use the terminology and techniques of that field in guiding clients toward settlement. The so-called transformative style of mediation emphasizes behavioral modification in addition to dispute resolution.

Some therapeutic mediators like to use a mediation technique that draws from their experience as family therapists. When mediating custody, they meet with the children to learn which parent they would prefer to live with; sometimes a child may be unaware that the parents are planning to divorce and needs to be told about the problems they have been having. These mediators believe people should be encouraged to discuss their feelings.

In one such case, neither of two children knew their parents were planning to separate, or even that a problem existed. When the mediator brought the parents and the children together to discuss the situation, she encouraged the parents to discuss their feelings. The children listened, for the first time hearing their parents talk about such things.

The father said that he had never been able to talk about how he felt. The mother described her impoverished childhood with an abusive and alcoholic father; she, her siblings, and her mother had banded together to protect each other and she had learned never to make demands for fear of putting even greater pressure on her mother. This habit had carried over into the marriage.

The mediator asked the father how he handled his feelings when his wife criticized him. He said that he withdrew into work and other activities, and eventually sought other women who expected less. Then the mother again described her disappointments, her attempts to communicate with her husband. She began to cry. Her daughter moved to her side. Her son looked at the floor.

The father cleared his throat and said, "I've never learned to talk about such things. That's why I am in therapy. I want us to be able to talk, so you can ask questions, so you will have a better chance to work things out than I did."

The mediator explained to the children that the separation had nothing to do with them, that both parents loved them. She discussed what their parents had been learning during the mediation. She asked the children to try to understand, and told them that divorce would not end their relationships with their parents.

The session did not end on a happy note; the entire family was silent. But the mediator felt that the problems had been properly aired. She believes such discussions are helpful. Ensuing sessions ironed out the details of the separation, but the mediator thought it equally important to help the clients regain respect and concern for each other.

This approach contrasts with that of divorce mediators who concentrate on the legal aspects of separation. Members of the therapeutic school delve into the emotional problems of the entire family, believing they are the crux of the problem. In this example, assuming that the mediator's analysis of the case was correct, her experience as a family therapist probably contributed to the mediation's ultimate success.

Therapy may not be the service some clients think they are purchasing, but it may nevertheless be in their best interests. When successful, the therapeutic approach provides valuable insights into clients' future needs, desires, and expectations. The multidimensional aspects of family disputes make this approach fascinating; resolving a family dispute this way may involve not only the usual reallocation of rights and responsibilities but the readjustment of relationships within the family.

The Communications School.   A family mediator is rarely aware of the complexities of a given case when clients come to their first session; for that matter, the clients may not be clear in their own minds about the issues that need to be resolved. Before these can be defined and agreed upon, the mediator has to gather information. Only after extensive fact-finding can the mediator begin to assist negotiations and forecast how disputes can be resolved.

Followers of the communications school believe that a primary duty of the family mediator is to provide the parties with information and guidance so as to develop their communications skills. Single mediators can do this, but sometimes a psychologist and lawyer team up. As in the therapeutic school, these mediators seek to create a more effective relationship between the clients.

In one case, Mabel and George headed a multinuclear family. Each had two children from prior marriages; Mabel's two teenagers lived with her and George, and George's kids lived with his former wife. On weekends, however, Mabel's children went to stay with their father and George's children came to stay with him and Mabel. It wasn't working. None of the children were happy. George said everything would have been fine if it weren't for Mabel's children. They talked about separating and ended up in mediation. At the first meeting they signed a retainer, but did not appear to have definite ideas about getting divorced.

The mediator invited Mabel's children to a joint session. The son said he wanted to live with his father because George was always criticizing him for not doing better in school. The daughter was noncommittal, but admitted she was unhappy. The mediator got permission to talk with George's children and his and Mabel's former spouses. After interviewing each on the telephone, he became convinced that the entire family was having trouble communicating with each other.

The mediator scheduled the next meeting without the children. Mabel began talking of her concerns about her daughter, but George frequently corrected her. She finally exploded, "Don't keep interrupting me all the time." She told the mediator George always did that. "With the kids, too. It drives them crazy."

The mediator asked Mabel to describe how that made her feel. She shrugged and looked toward her husband. He said, "I think she's trying to say that she'd rather speak for herself."

The mediator asked George whether that bothered him. "No," he replied. "I wish she could speak for herself. I think that's part of our problem. We don't talk about our feelings as much as we should."

The mediator suggested talking about how they expressed their feelings to each other and to their children. They agreed, so he helped them understand how to identify feelings and learn to express them, which led into a discussion of how they felt about their marriage. It became clear that they were still emotionally attached. Mabel deferred to her husband, who still felt responsible for her, and both loved all the children. It began to dawn on them that they liked being married. After several sessions, George and

Mabel decided to remain together, having recaptured the ability to communicate with each other.

Reconciliation is not the usual goal of mediators, who often expect only to help their clients separate amicably, but followers of the communications school find that their approach may indeed lead to reconciliation because they boost clients' communication skills.

Experienced mediators will know how to deal with whatever client issues are likely to surface. Sometimes communication is a problem, but more typical issues are parenting skills and the amount of family support payments and allocation of property. Often, the mediator will have to clarify the issues for the parties, since they are confronting them for the first time and have not considered them from all sides. The mediator's experience makes this possible.

The Ethics of Mediation

Mediation is a precarious profession because clients can withdraw at any time. Initial meetings are often consumed by persuading the parties to participate and explaining the conditions of the mediation so that they are fully understood and agreed upon before negotiating between the parties begins. Ethical problems may arise from the start; the mediator is dealing with potential clients who probably are not familiar with the mediation process. The mediator should emphasize the benefits of the process, of course, but also point out its risks and likely costs.

One mediator explains it this way: "The only advantage I have going for me is that I have been around this track many times before. I can explain situations, based on my experience. Unless [mediators are] familiar with the problems they are facing, the parties may decide that they can do just as well on their own."

A mediator must walk a tightrope, carrying clients on each shoulder. The clients may perceive mediation differently and be suspicious, reluctant to begin, or guarded. Discerning these attitudes quickly is a challenge for the mediator, but it must be done as a step toward convincing both potential clients to participate. The principle of informed consent is essential; the parties should know exactly what they are agreeing to. Chapter Three describes how this can be accomplished.

Ethical questions may arise at any stage of mediation. Some actions are obviously unethical and thus easy to avoid; they may violate professional standards of practice or be contrary to doctrines of civil (or even criminal) law. Mediators do not, of course, usually have to be told not to embezzle client funds or embark on a business relationship with a current client.

More enigmatic questions of ethics may arise when conflicts occur between the six principles of mediation mentioned earlier. For example, clients' rights to self-determination could conflict with the interests of their children. Dozens of such conflicts are described by Robert Baruch Bush (1992). A few of the more common ethical questions he mentions are these: What should a family mediator do when clients agree to enter into an unwise, unfair, or illegal contract? How should a mediator respond when one party lies, conceals information, or attempts to intimidate the other? Should a mediator try to protect a party who is being coerced into a settlement through ignorance, weakness, or fear? What should be done to protect the interests of children, other third parties, or the public?

These are difficult issues. Much as a mediator may be committed to impartiality, doing no harm, and party self-determination, dilemmas arise. The Academy of Family Mediators provides standards of practice, but family mediators still have to make difficult ethical decisions, often having to do with the prospect of intervening to protect clients' or other parties' long-term interests.

Another concern is the occasional conflict between the mediator's obligation to clients and the obligation to the process or to the community. Should confidentiality outweigh the otherwise clear need to notify a court or other authority if, for example, the mediator learns that the clients have agreed to some sort of illegal conspiracy? On the other side of that coin is the mediator who coerces or tricks clients to such an extent that they complain to the authorities themselves. Should a mediator be allowed to hide behind professional immunity? Those kinds of questions cannot be answered in general, but only for a given case after all relevant facts have been taken into account.

Problems During Mediation

Mediation is not free of risk, even though people can abandon the process at any time. An obvious danger is that a party might rush into an imprudent settlement. Mediation involves bargaining. To that extent, each party must be able to maintain a realistic position and not be swept away by emotions or the persuasiveness of the other party.

Differences in Negotiating Skills

Mediators cannot guarantee that neither party will make a mistake during negotiations. Usually the most a mediator can do is caution someone who appears to be caving in, but the process is driven by the parties, not the mediator. The terms of the settlement are their mutual responsibility.

A mediator is supposed to ensure balanced negotiations and not allow parties to manipulate or intimidate each other, but that does not mean a mediator should tell a party to reject an offer. Once a mediator concludes that someone is competent to participate in the negotiations, the primary responsibility shifts to that person, who then must accept the risk.

Of course, individuals are never exactly equal in negotiating ability, and a strong party may exploit the other's weakness. Some feminist critics of divorce mediation believe the process is unfair to women because it does not address the power imbalance between men and women (Grillo, 1991). They have a point. Mediators should do what they can to create a level playing field between the genders; at the very least, they should determine whether each participant is capable of negotiating with the other.

Making such determinations is discussed in Chapter Three, but parity between the sexes is a matter of debate within the profession. Some mediators worry considerably about maintaining a balance, while others believe their primary role is to bring about a settlement.

There is no foolproof system to ensure that parties do not make mistakes. Mediation is a human system based on compromise and collaboration. Sometimes settlements will later prove unwise. A separation agreement has to be submitted to a judge when the couple petitions for divorce, but no one would claim that such a review guarantees the fairness of the settlement. Family courts are too busy for more than a cursory appraisal of negotiated agreements.

In any event, not every mediated settlement is brought to court for review. For example, an agreement between brothers to share the cost of a nursing home for an aged parent, whether negotiated with or without the help of a mediator, would not require judicial review. That kind of agreement might not even be seen by an attorney. The involvement of a mediator may add some measure of protection, but does not guarantee that the agreement is fair. It is up to the parties to protect their own interests.

The Emotional Element

An initial question in every mediation is whether the participants have the intellectual and emotional capacity to negotiate. Some mediators try to combine mediation with therapeutic help, while others believe that people who cannot control their emotions should not be encouraged to mediate. Under any circumstances, mediators should ensure that each party is able to understand the implications and ramifications of what is being discussed. If necessary, a party should be referred to appropriate resources—therapy, for example—for help so that when negotiations do begin they can proceed in a fair and orderly way.

A person's lack of capacity may be permanent, perhaps because of mental illness or lack of intelligence, or temporary, as when a person is uninformed or under temporary stress. Mediators should be able to identify such problems and take remedial steps. If either party is unable to participate meaningfully in the process for any reason, the mediator may decide to suspend it and encourage the participant to seek help.

A mediator has some obligation to protect both parties, but that is a far cry from serving as an advocate for either. Observing that a woman seems to be less effective at negotiating than her husband, for example, does not give the mediator the obligation, or even the right, to represent her interests over her spouse's.

Bargaining power is based on control of resources, but may also involve intelligence, knowledge, personality, and hundreds of other factors. That a man has an assertive demeanor and controls the family checkbook does not necessarily mean he will dominate negotiations; his wife on the other side of the table may be equally or more assertive. Certainly one side or the other is likely to dominate in mediation, but usually a mediator should not do much about that other than stay neutral. So long as the weaker party is competent to participate, the mediator can allow the negotiations to continue. If one party seems to benefit more than the other from a settlement, so be it. A mediator is obliged to be neutral.

Family mediations often involve individuals who have lived together, but such intimacy can actually increase the possibility of emotional stress during mediation. Even a mediator who is not a trained therapist can usually tell when people's emotions are blocking their ability to negotiate. It is common; they may be angry or depressed, or have lost confidence in their ability to communicate. After many wrangles as their relationship careened down a long and contentious road, they may have stopped listening to each other and ceased trying to understand each other's needs and desires. In a family dispute, emotional pressure can lead to overwhelming despair with anger bubbling up from beneath the surface.

For some people, emotional displays are their customary way of communicating. Such a display may be a flag marking the source of the problem. Clients abuse each other; they yell, lose control, or storm out of the room because they may have no better way to communicate. Mediators must expect that kind of behavior and have ways to deal with it.

Anger, guilt, and alienation are common emotions among people seeking mediation. When family members don't get what they want, they may lash out at whoever seems to be in their way. They feel victimized, and the resulting anger may focus on immediate issues or be based on earlier incidents and controversies about which the mediator will likely be ignorant, as it is impossible for a mediator to know about every prior squabble. Parties come to mediation with a long history of disagreements trailing behind them.

Anger and guilt go hand in hand, reinforcing each other. The human mind tries to protect itself against feelings of guilt by finding someone else to blame. Because most people do not like to hold grudges against family members, they sometimes convert their anger at them into guilt, which manifests itself in sullen, misdirected unhappiness.

Family relationships are usually an important source of strength; thus loss of family can be devastating, particularly to individuals such as those going through separations, who are already worrying about finances, finding a new social life, fulfilling romantic needs, and taking care of children.

Losing family status often leads to alienation. A father who loses custody may no longer feel in control as a parent, and he may even abandon his children.

Loss of family threatens a person's identity. Loneliness and self-doubt color the world gray. The victim of a family controversy bathes in self-pity. Cut off from family, a person may drift into self-indulgence, eager to punish whoever seems responsible. One of the more difficult tasks of a family mediator is persuading participants not to blame the other party. Until they can get beyond that stage, negotiations can't be productive. Blame and other nonproductive emotions must be dealt with before settlement discussions can begin.

Mediators work through the clients and must keep their emotions under control. In one case, for example, the mediator was a psychologist who practiced family mediation. A postdivorce case came to her for mediation. The couple's separation agreement included an arbitration provision covering disputes over the son's education. The parties had gone to their arbitrator, but he encouraged them to mediate.

The initial session was rancorous. The mediator was appalled at the couple's hostility to each other; the father accused the mother of turning his son against him, and she said her son's problems were all caused by the father. They spent half an hour yelling at each other. Finally, the mediator refused to continue unless they stopped. For the next twenty minutes, she talked about their anger, explaining that their emotions had nothing to do with their son's education.

She persuaded them to concentrate on the schooling issue. At her suggestion, they each submitted a list of three acceptable schools. Then they eliminated one school from each list and agreed to submit applications to the other schools for the coming semester. If more than one school became available, they agreed their son would make the final choice. As it turned out, none of the schools had an opening for the boy, but they found and agreed on another school that did.

By helping her clients understand why they were fighting so bitterly, the mediator persuaded them to collaborate about their son's education. Why were they so angry at each other? The father wanted to reassert control over his son's life; the mother had not remarried and was still angry about being jilted. When they understood their emotions, they were able to reach a settlement.

Mediation, Arbitration, or Litigation?

All mediators have one thing in common: they mediate. They do not act as arbitrators or judges.

Arbitrators decide issues based on the evidence and on arguments made by advocates who appear before them. Arbitration is thus a form of adjudication. Mediation is not. Mediators do not decide cases, but rather help clients make their own decisions and settle their own issues.

Arbitration serves a specific purpose. When parties are unable to agree but don't want a judge or jury to decide the case, they can hire an impartial arbitrator to make a decision that all are required to follow. With mediation, however, the parties do not agree to abide by a third-party decision. Instead, they try to come to a decision between themselves, persuading, bargaining, and collaborating with each other under the mediator's guidance. Think about these differences. They are essential to understanding what is going on in family mediation.

Arbitration usually requires parties to retain lawyers to represent their interests, much as they would in court. The attorneys would argue to a judge if they were in a court; they argue to a different kind of decision maker in arbitration, but in either case they submit evidence and try to convince an adjudicator to decide in their client's favor. Litigation and arbitration have to do with obtaining decisions from someone else; mediation seeks decisions only from the parties in conflict.

Indeed, lawyers do not attend family mediation sessions in most parts of the country (there are exceptions, which will be discussed later), though they usually serve as outside advisers. They are seldom present even after mutual agreement has been reached by the parties involved, although a mediator may want to stay in touch with the clients' lawyers, if any, as the negotiations move forward.

Sometimes one or both parties will want to bring attorneys to a mediation session. Mediators handle that in different ways. In one case a wife wanted her lawyer present because she was afraid she would not be able to express herself well. The husband could have refused, but the mediator persuaded him to allow it as long as the lawyer did not speak without permission, and then told the wife that the session could be adjourned for a few minutes if she needed to talk to the lawyer. This worked reasonably well, and after the first session the wife felt comfortable being on her own.

As mediators do not make decisions for or against their clients, there is not much for attorneys to do at mediation sessions even if they attend. But if they do attend, as is often the case in business mediation, the tenor of the discussion is likely to be more formal, with more argument about legalities and more attempts by the lawyers to get the mediator to make rulings. It is the rare lawyer who will sit back and let the client talk.

Arbitration is a machine that generates private decisions. For some family disputes, it may be a good way to cut through the issues, but most parties would prefer to decide for themselves. No outsider can know as much as they do about their family.

If all attempts to negotiate settlement have failed, arbitration is still an option, and at that point it may be preferable to litigation, particularly if the arbitrator is trusted by both parties.

Contract clauses sometimes provide for arbitration instead of court action in the case of future disputes; this is common in separation agreements. As circumstances change, adjustments may have to be made in the terms of the agreement. A parent may lose a job or move to another community, with a resulting need to adjust visitation rights or the level of financial support. Even then, the parties should attempt to negotiate appropriate changes without arbitration. Usually, those kinds of problems can be worked out informally, perhaps with the help of a mediator. If not, the issue can be decided in accordance with the contractual arbitration clause. The arbitrator should be an expert on family law and whatever other issues are involved in the dispute.

When parties have been unable to reach an agreement but don't want a third party to make a binding decision, they may agree to obtain an opinion from a neutral expert. Such an opinion might be based on an independent investigation, on discussions with the parties, or on a formal hearing. Both parties should be involved in selecting the expert and assembling the information that will be submitted for consideration. In the postdivorce case above, for example, the parents might have asked a neutral consultant to recommend a list of schools for their son.

Sometimes advisory opinions are requested by family courts or by the parties' attorneys. Before agreeing to such a procedure, the parties should agree how the opinion will be used. Will each of them abide by it? If the opinion is binding, the procedure is essentially the same as arbitration. If it is not binding, it may be a waste of time.

Another alternative is for the parties to ask their mediator to decide whatever issues they are unable to resolve. If that authority is granted at the beginning of the mediation, it is called MEDARB, a combination of mediation and arbitration. Arbitration can also be agreed to after the parties have come to an impasse during mediation. They may ask their mediator to decide certain issues that they have not been able to resolve. At that stage, the arbitration can take place without a hearing and with no formalities.

An impasse-busting technique called MEDALOA combines the mediation process with last-offer arbitration. If, for example, the parties have been able to agree on every issue except the exact amount that one spouse must pay for child support, they can submit their final positions on that single issue in writing and agree to accept whichever one the mediator thinks is best. MEDALOA encourages the parties to close the gap between their final bargaining positions, because neither will want the mediator to select the offer of the other party. MEDALOA converts the neutral mediator into an impartial arbitrator, but with narrowly restricted authority.

MEDALOA seems preferable to open-ended arbitration because the parties do not have to give unlimited decision-making power to a third party. Like arbitration, MEDALOA generates decisions, but it more often results in the parties reaching settlement themselves. MEDALOA awards can be enforced in court, like an arbitration award.

Beyond the realm of both mediation and arbitration lies court. Many families continue to end up in family court, and many civil cases in state courts involve domestic relations issues of one kind or another. But whenever possible, family disputes should be resolved privately. Litigation is time-consuming and expensive, the atmosphere is oppressive, and the litigants and witnesses are likely to find the experience degrading. The testimony in domestic relations cases often discloses humiliating details of people's lives. Lawsuits can create family feuds that go on for generations. Talk to people who have been in litigation, or spend a day in a local family court; the experience will make it clear that public courts should be courts of last resort.

An article in the January 1, 1996 *New York Times* had this to say: "The matrimonial part is an intimate little viper's nest, where a lawyer's survival skills must include the art of fine-tuning a case to the quirks of whichever judge hears it. Judges have almost untrammeled power over the outcome of a contested divorce, and they can also order the spouse with the deeper pockets to pay for the other spouse's lawyer" (Hoffman, 1996). The article also quoted a lawyer: "They give very good attorneys' fees in New York County, so you could afford to put up a good fight for your client. Not like in Queens, where I've gotten $500 or $1,500 for a case. In Manhattan, they know the worth of a lawyer's time. You can get $15,000—real money" (Hoffman, 1996, p. 36).

Divorce lawyers are not much different in New York City than elsewhere: they are expensive. When the clients are of modest means, the fee for an noncontested divorce can be set in advance, but if the case is contested, the lawyers are paid by the hour. One way or another, the lawyers' fees must be paid. People who want to punish their spouses by piling up legal fees should remember that the money paid to attorneys will come out of what is available to support the family. There are seldom any real winners at the end of a contested divorce.

Not that lawsuits are never necessary. The prospect of being sued may bring a spouse to the bargaining table who otherwise might hang around long after the marriage is dead. Without access to the courts, some parties might not be able to force their spouses to negotiate.

Mediation may take place in the shadow of threatened litigation, but it offers both parties a chance to avoid that experience by working out their problems privately. Mediation does not eliminate the need for family courts but relieves them of many unnecessary cases, which is why family mediation is a public service. By helping to resolve disputes that might otherwise have to be decided in court, family mediators save the public money.

If a lawsuit does become necessary, both parties should retain attorneys who are experienced family court litigators. Even after they begin preparing the case for trial, it may still be possible to mediate some of the issues, although lawyers have a tendency to take control of a case; their involvement may reduce the likelihood of an early settlement. Most lawsuits do, however, get settled before trial. Unfortunately, by then expensive pretrial procedures may have already taken place, such as discovery, motion practice, and settlement conferences during which the lawyers jockey for position. Once the parties turn their case over to attorneys it may be too late to avoid the hostilities and expenses of litigation.

Most attorneys do their best to protect the interests of their clients. Some prefer to do that in court. Others are more settlement-minded. But the adversarial process itself creates problems. Each lawyer is expected to obtain every possible advantage, and they each want to win. The results can poison an already troubled family relationship, as the posturing of the adversarial process converts smoldering hostility into rage.

The late O. J. Coogler, one of the earliest enthusiasts of family mediation and author of *Structured Mediation in Divorce Settlements* (Coogler, 1978), was particularly critical of the role of lawyers in divorce negotiations. Coogler believed that divorce lawyers tended to take over control of their clients' case and to escalate the competitive struggle between them, limited only by the financial resources of the family. The anger and hostility that he experienced in his own divorce motivated him to create a more humane and rational method of resolving such disputes.

Some lawyers believe they have to fight for their clients by taking charge of negotiations, because they assume the clients are incapable of negotiating by themselves. Not surprisingly, when people retain such lawyers they almost always lose control and end up experiencing stress, bitterness, misunderstanding, and eventual shock at what happens to them in court.

Lawyers tend to emphasize financial matters at the expense of family relationships. They try to defeat opposing attorneys rather than encouraging couples to discuss their problems. Even clients who have formerly proved quite competent to handle their own affairs are told not to talk to their spouses. Some lawyers go so far as to advise pressuring spouses by cutting off support, taking money out of joint bank accounts, suspending mortgage and utility bill payments, canceling credit cards, and otherwise tightening the financial screws. A few even recommend threatening to take the kids away as a way of forcing the spouse to give up more property.

But many attorneys recognize that such adversarial approaches inhibit their ability to satisfy the needs of families. They understand that mediation may make it possible to obtain a good settlement without going to court. Still, some lawyers are not familiar with mediation and do not recommend it to their clients. Until recently, law schools did not cover mediation. Now, almost every law student is taught the basics of the mediation process, and more lawyers recommend it to clients.

Training lawyers to use mediation encourages its growth, which will reduce their tendency to favor litigation and improve the quality of life in our society. Mediation encourages interaction among people and empowers them to control their own lives. Mediation is now being recommended by many lawyers, and in Florida and Texas mediation is mandatory for all civil cases. Mediation is not only being used for family disputes but in employment, insurance, and general business to help disputants avoid court. Business attorneys have found that it resolves complicated disputes more effectively than either arbitration or litigation.

Summary

The American family is changing, which sometimes causes problems. Many of these problems can be ameliorated by family mediation that follows these basic values: decision making by the parties involved, informed consent, confidentiality, good-faith negotiation, the mediator's competence and impartiality, and consideration of the interests of other parties. Even so, these values sometimes conflict and create ethical problems for the mediator.

Various mediators subscribe to various schools of practice, but whatever techniques they use they are likely to encounter emotional and other problems of clients that hinder the mediation process, particularly in its early stages. However, clients can still learn how to collaborate and bargain effectively.

Family mediation is commonly used to help couples work out the terms of separation leading to divorce, but it can be used to settle other family disagreements. It has advantages over court litigation because it is less disruptive and allows the parties to resolve their own disputes.

Mediators must be fair and must help to produce informed and enforceable settlements that conform to domestic relations laws. Those laws are the subject of the next chapter.

Chapter Two

Family Disputes and the Law

A family mediator needs a working knowledge of family law, not to give legal advice but to identify legal issues that should be considered by clients and discussed by them with their attorneys. Some mediators give clients extracts from applicable state statutes and checklists that identify the issues that will need to be discussed and agreed upon.

Some family mediators are lawyers, but mediation is not the practice of law. There is a distinct difference between talking about the law with parties and giving a legal opinion. Mediators are asked questions about a broad range of subjects, including legal issues. Discussing the law is fine, but giving legal advice is the exclusive business of lawyers.

The Academy of Family Mediators advises mediators to provide information only in those areas where they are qualified by training or experience. That is a sensible suggestion, because one purpose of mediation is to help the parties reach an informed settlement.

The academy treats legal issues somewhat differently than other areas of expertise, reflecting the zealousness with which lawyers protect their exclusive right to practice law. When asked questions about legal rights or obligations, family mediators should advise the parties to seek independent legal counsel on those points before formalizing their final agreements. The academy places no such prohibition in other areas of expertise, such as property valuations, accounting, or family therapy. This reflects the academy's concern for protecting the legal rights of the parties and respecting the turf of the legal profession.

A mediator can talk about applicable law so long as those remarks are coupled with a suggestion that each party seek advice of counsel. This assumes both have retained attorneys or will do so before signing off on the settlement agreement, which is customarily the case in divorces but not necessarily in other areas of mediation. The parties may not want to hire a lawyer and may decide to rely on the mediator's opinion, but the mediator should point out that legal advice is not part of the service provided.

In nonlegal areas of expertise mediators can be more forthright, at least where they have adequate training or experience. If an opinion from an outside expert would be helpful, however, the mediator should encourage the participants to obtain it. Examples include property assessment, taxation, and family therapy. As with issues of law, the parties may prefer not to pay for separate opinions on these matters but to base their negotiations on the mediator's opinion and their own research. This is permissible, but mediators should not purport to be experts on such subjects when they are not.

A mediator should be cautious about volunteering opinions, particularly when a party will be relying on them. Training and experience are not enough; the opinion must be correct. If it turns out to be mistaken and one of the parties is damaged, that person may make a claim against the mediator. The argument that the mediator was providing only impartial mediation and not professional advice on every issue may work, but it still means mounting a defense.

One lawyer, trying his wings as a mediator, gave an informal opinion on federal tax law. The opinion turned out to be wrong, and one of the parties sued. The claim was denied in court based on language in the retainer agreement, but if the mediator had simply mentioned the problem up front and encouraged his clients to confer with their own tax advisers, he probably never would have been taken to court.

Domestic Relations Law

Domestic relations laws are always changing, often the result of unanticipated legislation. Thus family law is unpredictable. For example, the legal rights of women have expanded dramatically in recent years, and some traditional doctrines of family law have become obsolete.

Marriage itself has changed. In the Victorian era husbands dominated most families, in some senses virtually owning them. With some exceptions antiquated attitudes are no longer reflected in American family law; statutes generally reflect conventional legislative and judicial views of contemporary culture. There is a lag, however, because older men still dominate state legislatures and serve as judges in the family courts. An elderly legislator or judge may not have an up-to-date view of the modern family. Nevertheless, major cultural changes have been reflected in the domestic relations laws of the states and in the decisions of state court judges.

Marriage is intended to stabilize family life, providing for the economic and social needs of the members of the family and reinforcing cultural norms. That is why courts lend their support to the institution of marriage. In most ways, state legislatures are equally supportive. The state encourages stable marriages; after all, the alternative to private child support is welfare.

The Marriage Contract

Many people plunge into marriage with scarcely a casual concern about the consequences. But even in the United States, where divorce is generally available, marriage substantially changes the legal rights and obligations of individuals. The civil contract of marriage contains unusual characteristics. Consider the following:

- Almost any unmarried adult has the legal capacity to wed.

- Marriage creates legal rights and obligations that can't be transferred or assigned.

- Marriage can only be dissolved by death or by a court of competent jurisdiction.

- The marriage contract is intimate and ambiguous, largely based on implicit understandings.

The requirements of civil marriage may vary somewhat from the assumptions that a couple makes through religious betrothal, and neither the civil nor the religious marriage may reflect the emotional bonds between the couple.

Almost every bridal couple intends to create a lifetime partnership based on the mutual needs, expectations, and values they bring to the marriage. As the years pass and experience tarnishes each person's view of the other and of the external environment, the attitude toward the partnership may change. It would be astonishing if in the face of inevitable change marriage always continued to satisfy every couple. Some societies try to freeze people into their marriages, but in the United States, subject to various statutory formalities, unhappy couples are allowed to divorce. Many of them do.

It is still, however, easier to marry than to divorce. Why should this be? The state has an interest in encouraging marriage because the partners accept responsibility for each other and for their offspring. The institution of marriage relieves the state of substantial responsibilities. No wonder most governments make it easy to marry and harder to divorce. The law varies from state to state, but almost everywhere, marriage is easier to plunge into than to climb out of. If it were made even more difficult to divorce, however, fewer might marry in the first place.

A few states and an increasing number of religious organizations encourage couples to participate in prenuptial counseling, but most Americans can still get married with a minimum of delay, red tape, or consideration of the consequences. Arranged marriages, where families negotiate the conditions of betrothal, are not part of this culture no matter how sensible they might seem to many parents.

The Rights of Women

Under early common law, a married woman had relatively few rights. She could not enter into contracts. She could neither sue nor be sued. Her personal property became her husband's. If she wanted to engage in business, she had to do so as her husband's agent, using his credit and holding property in his name. Her children were primarily subject to the father's control. Some women became powerful, to be sure, but the law was an impediment to their progress.

A few countries still operate under such rules. Even in America, plenty of fathers expect to dominate their wives and children. There are many subservient mothers, many children who would hesitate to challenge their father's authority. Some wives knuckle under just as they might have in Victorian times, except that they are less likely to have servants and may be expected to go out and find work.

The gender equality struggle is not at an end. It was difficult even to win the basic legal rights for women that are in place today. The Nineteenth Amendment, which gave the vote to women in 1920, was an important step forward, as was the Civil Rights Act of 1964. Women had to assert themselves to achieve these milestones, and to their credit, they have more freedom and greater rights than ever before. It could be argued that without legal equality for women, family mediation would be inappropriate.

The battle goes on. On average, women still earn only about 70 percent of what men earn. In 1992, the median earnings of year-round, full-time workers was $30,407 for men and $21,747 for women (72 percent) (*Information Please Almanac*, 1996, p. 824). In politics, business, and higher education, women continue to be at a disadvantage. Cultural norms change slowly; individual attitudes and behavior may still fall behind the times.

A family mediator must appraise the relative power relationship of male and female clients and determine whether it is realistic to suppose that spouses can negotiate on equal terms. The same evaluation applies to nonspousal relationships, including child and parent. How equal are the relationships within a particular family? Can the members negotiate with each other?

There have been many debates on that issue, posed in generalities. The answer can only be found in terms of a particular dispute between particular parties. That is why the Academy of Family Mediators encourages mediators to ensure "balanced negotiations," whatever that means in a particular case. Obviously, no negotiations are perfectly balanced. The mediator must decide how much imbalance to allow.

Negotiations are always in flux. There are differences in the ability to persuade. Power pulsates for a myriad of reasons in family mediation as in other negotiations. What happens either at the table or away from it can tip the scales. The mediator may not even know what is happening, as relative power is internalized, tending to register in the minds of the parties. At most a reasonable balance may be possible, to the extent that a settlement can be reasonably fair under the circumstances. One participant may be handicapped by gender role, age, or dozens of other factors. Such a handicap should not be denied, because it may be reflected in the terms of any settlement.

Divorce

Divorce has become more acceptable in recent decades, and people who get divorced are seldom stigmatized. Part of the reason is that the grounds for divorce are no longer based on fault. Before that change in law, divorce had a bad name. One spouse had to be shown guilty of some sort of wrongdoing, such as adultery, desertion, or physical or mental cruelty, before a court would grant the other spouse a divorce. Each state specified its own grounds for granting divorce; some divorce laws were based on theology superimposed on the civil law.

Under those laws, even if both halves of a couple wanted to divorce they might have to provide proof of which partner was at fault for the failure of the marriage. State legislatures eventually concluded that such rigidity encouraged perjury; lawyers might "prove" adultery by having one of their clients "discovered" in bed with someone else. This was demeaning to everyone involved, including the judge who had to accept the testimony. Rather than participate in such a charade, many couples went to more lenient jurisdictions like Nevada or Mexico for a divorce.

In recent decades, almost every state has passed a no-fault divorce law, allowing couples to obtain a divorce whenever they agree that their marriage is dead, subject to various statutory conditions. The Uniform Marriage and Divorce Act (promulgated in 1970 and revised in 1973) contributed to the basis for many of those laws. A couple could show that their marriage was irretrievably broken by demonstrating that they have lived apart for the statutory period or by proving that serious discord existed between them. In some jurisdictions the courts might attempt reconciliations, but all were authorized to grant divorces.

Divorce laws still vary substantially. Some states kept the old grounds but added new ones. Others adopted versions of the Uniform Act. Family mediators should be familiar with the laws where their clients reside.

Incompatibility and irretrievable breakdown of the marriage are now common grounds for divorce. Most states accept them, but require the couple to live apart for a certain period of time, in some cases as long as three years. A divorce will be granted only if the couple have been living apart for the statutory period after duly executing a separation agreement that meets certain legal requirements. Some states require the parties to demonstrate an irretrievable breakdown in the marriage.

Couples who meet the statutory requirements can petition the court for a divorce decree based on the terms of their separation agreement. A hearing may be required, but not a contested trial. The judge will simply decide whether the separation agreement was entered into voluntarily and is generally in the public interest.

Many Americans believe that couples should be allowed to obtain a divorce when they are no longer compatible, that family assets should be fairly divided, that reasonable support payments should be made, and that children should be allowed to continue to associate with both parents. But how should these notions be applied to a particular case? Couples who have been living apart and petition the court for divorce can obtain relief, but unless they are able to agree on the terms, the court will decide. Judges have substantial discretion in allocating responsibilities between individuals, but they generally respect voluntary arrangements negotiated by the parties themselves. It is possible in this way to dissolve a marriage without becoming involved in a court contest over which party was responsible for its failure.

Recently, a few no-fault laws have been criticized for making it too easy to obtain a divorce, based on concerns that some spouses and children are being cast adrift without adequate resources. Part of this backlash comes from conservative religious groups who say that liberal divorce laws threaten family values, making it too easy for couples to slip out of their marriages.

Family Courts and Divorce

In most states the family court must approve separation agreements entered into as part of divorce decrees. If the parties are unable to come to terms on their agreement, the dispute can be decided by a family court judge. The court is armed with the power to compel a party to participate, an unattractive prospect that motivates some reluctant parties to mediate. This explains why not everyone who attends a mediation session does so with enthusiasm: some are there only because of the threat of litigation. A mediator can usually identify them, and should then be wary; they may be unwilling to bargain in good faith.

To help deal with unwilling participants, mediators should be familiar with the procedures and policies of their local family courts and have a working knowledge of how cases are processed there.

They are then equipped to persuade clients that court is not the best place to resolve problems. Forced to compare what happens in court to what takes place in mediation, clients usually choose to continue in mediation.

A court trial can become a pitched battle. The lawyers do all the talking; the clients are spectators, watching their private lives on display. When they do testify, the opposing lawyer will cross-examine them, asking unpleasant personal questions and perhaps attempting to show that they are lying.

Family therapists are often expert witnesses in contested divorce cases. One psychologist who has participated in many trials described what happens in court: "When I establish my professional credentials in court and then pontificate about what I think might be best for a child, I sometimes become alarmed because the judge has no other basis for a decision. I am controlling the case. My judgment is being imposed upon the family, a sobering idea. What do I know about what they want to make of themselves? How do they really feel about their kids? I wish that I could sit down with them and take the time to talk about it. The system doesn't work that way."

Some authorities believe that divorce courts give too much weight to the opinions of such experts. The use of experts also increases legal costs and may reinforce the parties' antagonism. This is particularly true of contested child support cases, where courts and social service agencies sometimes intervene in the lives of children and adults. When litigation results from such interventions, the legal costs and disruption in the participants' lives can breed even more antagonism. The investigation that precedes the hearing may also pit one parent against the other.

Family courts have broad jurisdiction. They must decide what to do about children whose parents are unable or unwilling to care for them. When a child is institutionalized or placed in foster care, the parental relationship is diminished; children removed from their homes for undetermined periods may never return. A court may later inquire about the biological family, but by then it may be too late. Many children remain in limbo, with their natural families destroyed.

There are plenty of opportunities for court intervention in family life. Almost two million children are in foster care, often because their custodial parent or parents are unable to carry out their responsibilities to them. The primary obligations of family courts are toward children. Difficult judicial decisions have to be made about them based on professional opinions that may be at odds with the preferences of the natural parents. The system imposes an adversarial approach, even though social service agencies do their best to provide counseling. When issues of child welfare arise, it is difficult to forecast the result. Judges consider the child's need for permanence and for parents, but what does this mean when dealing with real people?

Family cases are tough. They provide more than enough headaches for family courts, which is why judges are delighted when couples are able to negotiate settlements and why they encourage private mediation.

The Hot Button: Custody

Many years ago, courts gave custody to fathers on the theory that they owned the children. Then the pendulum swung the other way, tending to award custody of children, especially young children, to the mother. Now most courts take what they perceive as a more humane approach and attempt to determine the best interests of the children. State law may contain certain standards that judges must consider. These may be based on the Uniform Marriage and Divorce Act, but there are important differences between the various state laws. Some consider the wishes of the children, but other factors may be equally important. One court may consider the parents' religious views and their impact upon the child. Another may hold that intimate relationships between a parent and another person should be considered, whether heterosexual or homosexual. Mediators need to be familiar with the state laws their clients must adhere to.

Custody contests in court often degenerate into agonizing battles between the attorneys, as each submits testimony from mental health experts and others. In determining the best interests of the children, the judge may have to choose between dramatically conflicting expert opinions. The adversarial atmosphere of litigation emphasizes the parties' differences. The judge may be under pressure to decide quickly because of a backlog of cases.

Unlike a public judge, a mediator can take more time, encouraging the parents to collaborate rather than enter into a contest. The emphasis in mediation is on encouraging parents to agree on what is best for their children.

In *Ford* v. *Ford*, Justice Black of the United States Supreme Court said, "Unfortunately, experience has shown that the question of custody, so vital to a child's happiness and well being, frequently cannot be left to the discretion of parents. This is particularly true where, as here, the estrangement of husband and wife beclouds parental judgment with emotion and prejudice" (371 U.S. 187 [1962]).

The issue of what is best for the child may come before a judge like Justice Black, who would discount the opinion of the parents. Many parents would prefer to decide such issues for themselves. A mediator would encourage them to regard themselves as partners in child rearing and to take advantage of their right to design whatever arrangement best meets the family's needs; failing to do so could lead a judge to take that privilege out of their hands.

The law imposes an obligation upon parents to support their children. Various laws define that obligation in terms of child support guidelines. The application of these standards to a particular family by a judge should be based on a knowledge of the family, and therein lies the problem: there is seldom enough time for a judge to develop such knowledge. In court, time is severely limited by the pressure of other cases, but in mediation the parties can discuss the issues at length.

Before family responsibility laws were passed, the husband had the primary obligation to support the family. Now most state laws attempt to equalize the burden by also imposing it on the wife.

While the family is living together, the appropriateness of its standard of living is regarded as a private matter to be determined by the parents. The level at which they support their children is not generally subject to review, so long as the family is intact. That is not to say that disputes do not arise. From the time a child is first given pocket money until the child becomes independent, there may be family disagreements over the allowance. Sometimes these payments are contingent upon the child submitting to parental regulations. Informal agreements as to such rules are negotiated and renegotiated in most families.

The parents' legal obligation continues until the child reaches maturity. Even after that, some jurisdictions impose a continuing duty to support a retarded child or one requiring unusual medical care. Even if there were no legal obligation, moral commitments within the family often provide the foundation for continuing negotiations.

A myriad of potential disagreements can arise when parents refuse to pay the educational or medical expenses of their children. A negotiated settlement is preferable to litigation. A mediator may suggest ways to resolve the problem or at least focus the parties' attention on options that might make a settlement possible. When these kinds of disputes go to court, the participants may be forced to disclose embarrassing details about their relationship. Most families prefer to avoid this by resolving their internal disputes privately, working out a reasonable solution based on the needs and desires of the participants.

Agreements to support stepchildren also create disputes. If a stepparent's agreement to support the child is not in writing, it may be unenforceable. If the couple later separates, the obligation of the stepparent may terminate. In the case of couples who are not married, the relationship between the child and the natural parent's companion may be even more tenuous.

The powers and duties of parents include the right to bring up and control the child and the obligation to feed and clothe and house the child, providing health care and education. Some responsibilities can be delegated to others, but the primary duty remains with the parents, or the parent who has custody. As part of a separation or divorce, legal or de facto custody may be awarded to one or both of the parents. Custody is defined by state statute.

A parent who has not been awarded custody may be watching with a critical eye, ready to petition the court if there are signs that the child is not being properly cared for. Such a parent may have visitation rights, which make it easier to monitor the situation. This kind of dispute is common and can be resolved in mediation, with the court involved only to the extent of confirming whatever the parties are able to decide.

If the parent with legal custody decides to move away, the other parent may attempt to block it, perhaps on the basis that access to the child will become impossible. A judge may have to decide whether the move is being made for legitimate reasons, whether it is in the best interests of the child, and whether it interferes with the petitioner's access to the child.

One New York judge refused to permit a woman to take her child to Las Vegas to start a career as a singer, but other courts have allowed moves to accept a new job or join a new spouse. Mediators need to know how such cases have been decided in their clients' jurisdictions.

A judge may award custody of young children to one parent and order the other to pay child support, or order some version of joint custody. If the parties are unable to agree, the judge will have to exercise discretion.

There is a close relationship between custody and child support because caring for a child can be expensive. Child support is supposed to balance need and ability to pay. Many states have adopted child support guidelines. Nevertheless, it is sometimes difficult to estimate how much a particular judge will award. Too little and the children will suffer; too much and the noncustodial parent may be staggering under an impossible burden. The unpredictability of judicial decisions has encouraged many couples to negotiate settlements on their own.

Divorce lawyers try to calculate in advance what a particular family court judge is likely to allow. That becomes the basis for their negotiations. Those figures can be helpful when parties are attempting to mediate a dispute. If the parties have retained lawyers to represent them in court, a mediator might suggest that they obtain such estimates from their attorneys. A mediator may have enough knowledge of the local judges to provide the same calculations, which might be helpful in determining whether the parties are talking in realistic terms.

Most judges believe that children should continue to have contact with both parents. This has resulted in an increasing number of orders for joint custody. The Uniform Child Custody Jurisdiction Act (promulgated in 1968 and broadly adopted by states) has attempted to rationalize this area of the law, but it continues to be a controversial area.

Visitation Rights

The noncustodial parent usually obtains visitation rights. Disputes may arise when a parent violates the terms of visitation, perhaps by failing to return a child. Many states have passed versions of the Uniform Child Custody Jurisdiction Act, which is intended to deter child abductions by noncustodial parents and to provide interstate assistance in adjudicating custody cases by eliminating "jurisdictional competition and conflict with courts of other states." That law puts teeth into whatever limitations on access have been placed in the separation agreement. The Federal Bureau of Investigation is authorized to investigate and prosecute kidnappings by parents; according to the Department of Justice thousands of such abductions take place each year.

Child Find of America was established to assist custodial parents when a noncustodial parent abducts a child. The organization has been able to locate many children and return them to the custodial parent, and has established a mediation program to help resolve such situations. An examination of this program's cases reveals how desperate some parents become in the turmoil of a battle over custody, making the case for mediation all the more compelling.

For the parent who has not been awarded custody, continuing contact with the child is defined by the visitation rights in the separation agreement. If that issue is decided in court, the judge may exercise discretion, but will often give the noncustodial parent the right to be with a child during some defined period.

When visitation rights are negotiated by lawyers, they may view it as one of several secondary issues that they must haggle over, one lawyer demanding maximum visitation time and the other offering limited time. In the end, they may recommend a compromise to their clients. For example, if one parent seeks weekly visitation and the other monthly, the lawyers may press the couple to accept every other weekend.

Lawyer-to-lawyer bargaining may not result in as flexible or realistic a formula as the parties might have worked out for themselves with the help of a mediator. Visitation provides an opportunity for the noncustodial parent to create a wholesome relationship with the children, something that should be talked out in a collaborative way by the parents rather than bargained over by their lawyers. The parents should be encouraged to consider all of the alternatives, particularly where both are willing to share responsibility for their child.

Children who have been involved in a divorce often express the wish for greater contact with their absent parents. Most children are unhappy if they hardly ever see their noncustodial parents; they usually want more such contact and want it for many years after divorce. Otherwise they may later resent the restrictions imposed by visitation schedules created by lawyers, especially when the schedules are strictly policed by one of the parents. When a child constantly hears the custodial parent carping over such things with the other parent ("You were twenty minutes late today, and last week you came back before you were supposed to; we can't go on this way"), it is easy to see where things are headed. It will create tensions between the parents and diminish the pleasure that the children would otherwise derive from visitation.

Sometimes other relatives want contact with the children. Grandparent visitation laws are in place in most states, and courts enforce them. For example, an Illinois court ruled that the parents of a deceased mother had the right to see her child. Other state courts have done the same.

Why do those kinds of issues have to be resolved in court? Some separation agreements provide visitation rights for the grandparents, but most such situations are handled informally. As a mediator, one might ask the parties whether they anticipate that their parents or other close relatives will want access to the children. Perhaps that should be part of the separation agreement. The parties can avoid future squabbles with each other's relatives by planning for them in advance. When a dispute arises between one party and the other's parents or other relatives, mediation may be appropriate; it can help resolve a wide range of family disputes and need not be limited to separation agreements.

Alimony

Divorce courts decide claims for alimony based on the needs of the spouse seeking support and the financial resources of the other party. Other factors considered are the length of the marriage, the age and health of the parties, their earning potential, and their level of education. Some judges also consider the circumstances surrounding the divorce. For example, a woman who had committed adultery was denied alimony by a South Carolina judge.

Some husbands have been awarded alimony; as a result of the 1979 Supreme Court decision in *Orr* v. *Orr*, most states have taken gender out of their alimony laws.

Parties should consider the income tax consequences of describing support payments as alimony or child support. Alimony may be deducted from taxable income if the separation agreement provides that the payment does not continue after the death of the spouse and if the couple are not living together and are separated under a decree of divorce when the payment was made. Spousal support payments can be structured in many ways. For example, payment can be in a lump sum, or periodically as an annuity that may continue until some defined future time or event. Alimony provisions may specify that payments will end if the ex-spouse remarries, but if the payment is part of a property settlement that may not be the case. When the recipient simply moves in with another partner the obligation to pay alimony does not usually end. This may infuriate the former spouse, who may simply stop sending checks. A private detective hired by ex-husbands in such cases says, "Sometimes the woman has to take my client to court. My guy is outraged when a judge tells him to pay the money. He can't believe that he has to pay for some other guy's pleasure. That is how he sees it."

A few states terminate alimony if the recipient lives with another partner *and* it results in improved financial circumstances. Forecasting the outcome of such a case requires a close reading of court decisions dealing with similar facts.

The parties should decide whether support payments will be subject to adjustment in the event of some future contingency. If the payer's financial situation changes, the payments might be subject to renegotiation. How should those adjustments be determined? A Wisconsin man who won $19 million in a lottery shortly after his divorce was ordered to pay part of his winnings to his former wife. How would that contingency have been handled under a mediated agreement?

Some agreements contain arbitration clauses to deal with these contingencies. Arbitration allows the parties to resolve issues without going to court. If unable to agree, they can ask an arbitrator to decide for them. The award will be binding, except that some states may assert the right to review awards that relate to custody.

Enforcing Family Support

A major area of legislative concern has been how to determine appropriate levels of child support and how to enforce those obligations. The Child Support Recovery Act of 1992 made it a federal crime to fail to pay support for a child in another state, but the enforcement problem continues to exist. It is not much easier to collect support payments today than it was before the change. Many parents hold back payments or simply default. Some studies indicate that parents who are paying under a mediated settlement are more likely to pay than those ordered to pay by a court (Pearson and Thoennes, 1989). As Joan Kelly explains, "Mediation contains rather than escalates conflict, facilitates more positive postdivorce parental communications, and enhances compliance with agreements" (Kelly, 1993, p. 150). A separation agreement can be frustrated by someone who refuses to abide by its provisions. There is no point in negotiating with someone like that. Clients should be warned that the value of any settlement depends on both parties being willing to meet their obligations.

The legal remedies for enforcing child support are cumbersome. Court processes generally require that a lawyer be retained, but a party seeking to enforce such an obligation may not be able to afford it. The legal system does not provide an efficient method for extracting periodic payments from reluctant defendants, whether they stubbornly resist complying or simply are difficult to locate.

Some who owe support conclude that the system is so cumbersome that they will never be forced to pay by anyone; those who are owed money may find it easier to go on welfare than to sue for payment. Congress has attempted to assist in the collection process by making it easier to locate an absent parent, with the federal government assuming most of the cost of administration. States have established enforcement programs too, but child support remains difficult to collect, particularly when the debtor has moved away.

In spite of the efforts of the Organization for the Enforcement of Child Support, which tries to locate delinquent parents and lobbies for more effective laws, many parents who are supposed to receive child support from their former spouses don't receive the full amount. For many others the payments come in late or only after lawsuits have been filed.

Mediators should bear this problem in mind. If a mediator suspects that someone is not going to make payments, the custodial parent should be warned of those concerns. Sometimes it may be possible to secure payment in advance through escrow funds or to capitalize the obligation through an annuity or a mortgage on real estate. A payment in hand is better than an obligation from someone unwilling to pay.

Most states authorize collection through the attachment of wages or pension benefits or a payment into court. Some have tied nonpayment into cancellation of a driver's license. A provision in the Employment Retirement Income Security Act prohibits assignment of covered benefits by anyone other than the worker. An ex-spouse may be unable to touch those payments, particularly if the retired spouse has remarried. Family mediators need to be familiar with the problems involved in collecting support payments.

Support obligations that are reasonable are more likely to be paid. Their value depends upon whether the payments will be made. Regardless of what the law or the separation agreement says, the attitude of the payer will determine whether the obligation is met. The recipient should bear this in mind before making it difficult for the payer to continue seeing the children. Turning the children against that person may reduce the likelihood of continued payment. A parent who is encouraged to maintain an active parental role is more likely to comply with the obligation to support the children.

How parents cope with their divorce may have an effect on their children and on support. By encouraging the children to have frequent and enjoyable visits with the other parent, the custodial parent can help ensure that the children will not be deprived of an important relationship and that support payments will come in on schedule. Otherwise, a noncustodial parent may feel rejected and decide to stop sending checks, a scenario that is neither in the child's interest nor that of the custodial parent.

Nonsupport is not the only difficult problem. The parent who has been given custody may abandon the child or attempt to invalidate the custody agreement in court. If a custodial parent fails to provide care, the other parent may have to take back the child. This is not as common as the failure to pay child support, but it does happen. Parties need to be made aware of these contingencies. It is up to the mediator to enlighten them about some of the risks that they will be assuming under their separation agreement.

Nonsupport may even cause the custodial parent to become unwilling to care for the child. A mediator should explain that a separation agreement contains reciprocal obligations. For the agreement to succeed, both parties must understand that they will be relying on the continuing performance of the other.

In that sense, a separation agreement is like a long-term labor contract. The parties anticipate that it will stay in effect for many years, during which the fortunes of the participants are likely to change in unexpected ways. It is sensible to try to anticipate whatever problems may arise. The analogy to a labor contract is not far-fetched. One parent agrees to care for the child, and the other agrees to provide some or all of the means for that care.

Separation agreements are particularly fragile because they are subject to changing circumstances. Some parents cut and run. Others suffer serious financial setbacks. Death, disability, and other unanticipated events may occur. Parties who agree on a formula for their future today may feel quite differently tomorrow. They may be unable or unwilling to live up to their contractual obligations. That is why it is important for parties to achieve a relationship during the mediation that encourages collaboration and to plan in advance how disputes will be resolved in the future.

Other Family Legal Issues

State laws cover the issues of custody, child support, and alimony already discussed. They also deal with property allocation, separation agreements, and other matters.

Property Rights

Some state statutes provide that all property acquired during a marriage shall be divided between divorcing people in accordance with a certain formula, unless they agree to different arrangements. That formula must be well understood by mediators in the area to which it applies.

Under no-fault divorce laws a judge has broad discretion. If the parties come to court with a negotiated separation agreement, judges usually grant a divorce in accordance with its terms. In that way, a separation agreement can expedite the divorce; it is the link between divorce and a petition for divorce. By helping the parties reach agreement, a mediator facilitates the work of their attorneys. The mediator does not file the divorce petition, but should be familiar with what a separation agreement must contain in order for it to be accepted by the court.

In the absence of an agreement, a judge will divide the marital property, including real estate and intangible property such as bank accounts, securities, and income from a business or pension. Determining marital assets and allocating them between the parties can be decided by the parties themselves or by a court.

The Separation Agreement

Separation agreements vary by case. State law may require certain standard provisions, but the parties themselves should identify the agreements that need to be included. In general, separation agreements allocate property, determine financial support for the children and the dependent spouse, and arrange for child custody. The document should also include whatever other terms and conditions the parties may require to regulate their future relationship with each other and with their children. Separation agreements between a couple with children usually include at least the following provisions:

- An agreement to live apart
- A division of property, real and personal
- The amount of alimony, if any
- The arrangements for custody and child support
- The allocation of medical and educational expenses
- Provisions for taxes and insurance

The various fees and expenses of the mediation itself may be covered in a separate agreement. The hourly rate should have been established at the first session and incorporated in a retainer agreement. The payment can be handled in various ways, either shared equally between the parties or allocated in some other acceptable way.

If a divorced couple remarry, their separation agreement automatically comes to an end. A reconciliation may also void their contract, absent a provision that covers such an eventuality. Mediators may want to warn clients about that.

There are other peculiarities about separation agreements. If the agreement "induced" a divorce, it may be unenforceable. The law has its mysteries and this is one of them, but here is an explanation. Most separation agreements anticipate a divorce, but if the agreement was based on a promise to divorce, it may be voidable because it has induced the divorce. For example, if one of the parties was persuaded to sign on the basis of a lump sum payment, that person may later claim to have been induced and attempt to void the agreement. This aspect of the law is generally to be found in court decisions, not in the statutory law. For mediators who are not attorneys, one of the more difficult subject areas is the common law of domestic relations, that is, the law that does not appear in the statute books but can only be discovered by reading the appellate decisions of the state courts. Mediators who are not attorneys should study a textbook on local family law.

A chronic problem with the courts is how long it takes to reach a final a decision. The appeals may leave the parties in limbo for extended periods. When the case involves the rights of children, such long-drawn-out litigation may result in alienation and bitterness.

Family disputes can be further complicated when more than one jurisdiction is involved. For example, one state court might award custody to a mother, but a court in another state might award custody to the father on the basis that the mother's religious views might have a negative impact on the children. Imagine how much money would be wasted in that kind of litigation.

Homosexual Parents

Some judges believe that homosexuality detracts from a parent's ability to bring up a child, but there is no unanimity on that score. Other judges would be more likely to base their decision on the evidence that the woman is a devoted mother and a fit parent than whether she might be a lesbian. The cases go both ways, but one state judge gave custody to a father because the mother was living with another woman in a homosexual relationship and said that lesbians are not "normal." Another denied custody to a mother because of an open homosexual relationship; she and another woman had been living together with their sons, and even though a psychiatrist testified that a boy raised in such a home was unlikely to become homosexual and recommended that he be left with his mother, the court denied custody.

Not every judge is biased against homosexuals, but it is difficult to anticipate how a particular judge will react. Divorce lawyers know that every judge harbors certain individual prejudices, which must be considered when presenting their cases. Parties who suspect that a family court judge may be hostile can avoid risking their case by reaching a private settlement with the help of an impartial mediator.

Community Property

The community property concept came from civil law based on the Code Napoléon that was transplanted from Europe and Latin America into the newly created states in the Southwest. Those and a few other states adopted community property laws, which classify property as "separate" or "community." A married couple acquire an undivided interest in property that they obtain during their marriage, but maintain their individual ownership of separate property that one of them acquired before the marriage or after it was dissolved.

Many forms of property may be involved, such as compensation, rents, profits, or court awards. The classification process is complicated. For example, gifts and inheritances may be separate even though they were received by an individual during the marriage. One court found that calves born during the marriage were community property even though the cows that bore them were owned by the husband prior to the marriage.

Other questions arise. Can property be transferred from one category to the other by private agreement? What are the restrictions on the use of community property? If property is in more than one state, which state's law applies?

These questions have important legal and tax implications for married couples in community property states. A divorce may terminate the marital relationship but unleash many thorny questions of ownership. Mediators in those states need to know the community property law.

It is often difficult to identify community property rights. For instance, a spouse who has paid for a partner's professional training during the marriage may be entitled to a fair share of whatever earnings result, even after a divorce. As one California judge explained, the beneficiary of the training would otherwise walk away from the marriage with a windfall that might have great value. Similar findings have come down in several other states.

Equitable Distribution

Many states have passed "equitable distribution" laws that attempt to create fairness standards for allocation of marital property in the event of separation or divorce. These statutes vary in detail, but generally attempt to define the factors that should be considered by a court in allocating property.

New statutory language always poses a challenge for the courts. These statutes are still being clarified. For example, in Pennsylvania the law contained ten factors to be considered in dividing property, including length of the marriage, the age and health of each party, and their sources of income. The statute did not specify how much weight should be given to each factor, so one early decision said that they should be given equal weight.

Equitable distribution laws may increase litigation, at least until it becomes clear how courts will interpret the language. But they may also encourage parties to negotiate property settlements privately, not knowing how a judge might rule. If their case went to court, the application of the complex statutory standards might mean that just gathering the necessary information would drag on for months.

Equitable distribution requires that a value be assigned to each piece of property. In mediation, the parties can determine how their residence is evaluated—appraised value, fair rental value, or market value. They can calculate their own interest in a mortgage, and decide whether a rent-free home is credited toward alimony or family support. These are complex questions, and the parties will need advice before entering into their final negotiations. In states that have adopted equitable distribution, mediation may be particularly attractive, but the parties will want to know how a court might allocate their property. A mediator should be prepared to discuss the various options in a realistic way.

Tax Considerations

Tax considerations can be an important aspect of the negotiations leading to a separation agreement. The tax implications of allocating alimony, child support, and the transfer of property can be complicated. Alimony payments are deductible, but may be taxable income to the recipient under certain circumstances. It is important that the parties know in advance whether their settlement will qualify for favorable tax treatment.

Support is usually paid periodically. A lump sum payment may have a different tax impact. The situation can get even more complicated when trusts are used to cushion the impact of the settlement. Parties should be advised to discuss the formula with a tax adviser before signing their agreement.

The Internal Revenue Code allows taxpayers to allocate the tax burdens associated with their separation. The parties and their advisers can structure the financial arrangements to their advantage. No property settlement can be discussed intelligently without some consideration of the tax implications. Tax management can reduce the out-of-pocket costs for one party and give the other some tax-free income. A mediator should not only be familiar with income tax considerations but have some familiarity with gift and estate taxes.

Unmarried Couples

Even unmarried couples may acquire mutual obligations. In a well-publicized California case, an unmarried woman who had lived with movie star Lee Marvin for about seven years claimed half the property he had acquired during that period, plus support payments. California is a community property state. She claimed that

Marvin had agreed to compensate her, but his lawyer argued that the relationship was null and void because it was based on an immoral relationship. Initially her claim was denied, but when the case was sent back to trial after appeal, a judge decided the defendant had to pay $104,000 to rehabilitate the plaintiff's career. That case added the word *palimony* to the English language. Spouses may claim alimony, but an unmarried companion may demand palimony ("Obituary of Lee Marvin," 1987).

A mediator for a marital separation should also bear in mind that one or both clients may be living with someone new. What part will that person play in the settlement?

At one time, men who reneged on agreements to marry could be sued for breach of promise. Most states have excluded that theory of action. However, money paid to a fiancé in "expectation of marriage" may still be recovered if the wedding is canceled. Sometimes the process of untangling such a couple's assets may require extensive negotiations at a time when the couple are no longer on speaking terms. A mediator might be helpful. More and more couples are living together without being married, so these sorts of disputes will continue to surface.

Relationships can become complicated. In one situation, a man invited his first wife to move back into his home. They had been divorced for several years and he was still married to his second wife. "Sure," his first wife said, "but first divorce your second wife, then give me a salary and an equity interest for the work I will be doing for your business." After they lived together for five years on that basis, they split up again. She filed a claim for community property. The court rejected her claim because she had been living with him as an unmarried person, not as his wife. Property acquired during unmarried cohabitation does not become part of the community property, even though they had once been married.

A question that has attracted recent attention concerns the legal rights of homosexual couples. Are they equivalent to those of married couples? The trend may be toward recognizing such relationships. A mediator should be aware that some clients may have already accepted such concepts. Just as some people's attitudes lag behind social and legal changes, some clients have accepted ideas that are not yet part of the state statutes.

Summary

As couples dance their minuet of marriage, separation, and divorce, their legal rights will need to be sorted out. Usually they are able to settle their differences after some wrangling, but some decide they need family mediation to help them. Only the most intractable conflicts should be taken to court.

Family law, based on state statutes and court cases, is unpredictable because it gradually changes to reflect contemporary mores. In spite of the passage of uniform laws and the imposition of certain federal standards in areas of national concern, every state's law is different. Attorneys who specialize in family law will be familiar with the peculiarities of their own state. Most of them limit their practice to a single jurisdiction. A family mediator needs to be able to talk the same language. Family mediators also tend to work within a single jurisdiction.

This chapter has only touched upon some of the primary issues that are likely to arise in family mediation. Family mediators should be familiar with their local laws, not to give legal advice but to recognize the legal issues that their clients may encounter.

Chapter Three

Family Mediation in Action

This chapter explains how mediation works and how mediators help clients resolve disputes. People are usually in mediation because they have distressing problems. Under stress, they often do strange things. They break into tears, yell at each other, snarl threats across the negotiating table, even run out of the negotiating room. They may even destroy lifelong relationships with ill-timed bursts of invective. Mediators sometimes may wonder if they are the only rational people involved; clients may become unaware how their antics appear to others.

In business negotiations, parties are usually represented by more or less equally competent people and are committed to fairly realistic goals. This may not be so in family disputes, where the negotiators are likely untrained and intensely emotional. The adversaries may be at loggerheads because they no longer listen to each other or are so angry that they can't begin to compromise. The family mediator's job is to deal with such problems.

In a sense, family mediation is not an entirely rational process. If rational behavior is consistent and intended to fulfill established aims, many mediating parties are not completely rational. People are never totally consistent; everyone holds a few ideas, beliefs, and desires that are inconsistent with each other, and their aims shift from moment to moment as opportunities arise and situations develop. These inconsistencies in the family mediator's work environment are not always a negative factor. The mediator can use the parties' willingness to be inconsistent to bring them together.

People want to appear consistent, however, which is why they attach themselves to their opinions and hold on. When they come to a mediation, they usually have fixed notions of what will happen. As each person's position is generally based on self-interest, parties in mediation are likely to start off far apart. The mediator must make widely differing positions converge. This can only be done by creating inconsistency, moving the parties one step at a time from their extremes toward a center where they can reach settlement.

At the Beginning

What brings people to mediation in the first place? Many things, but it is not unusual for one side or the other to refuse mediation at first or even to deny there is a problem. Often only an explosive event of some kind will jar them into action.

"I can't live this way any longer and I've talked to a divorce lawyer" is the sort of declaration of marital war that can start a couple down the road to mediation, especially if followed by words such as: "Either we fight this out in court or try to come to some agreement. For the sake of the kids, let's go to a mediator." Perhaps half the time, the other party will agree.

Sometimes violence is the trauma that brings a reluctant party to the table. More than a few couples have decided to separate in the aftermath of a drunken brawl that ended with them trading blows or wrestling on the kitchen floor. Other couples recognize the depth of their alienation only when a child runs away from home. Then it is time to talk, so that everyone can try to understand what has gone wrong.

Before mediation proceeds, it is important to consider the physical setting of meetings between mediator and clients. Parties may be under stress when they come together, so a comfortable, informal setting is appropriate. This is particularly true for the initial meeting, when the parties are sizing up the mediator. Some mediators like to meet around a table in a conference room. Others believe that a table hinders communication and prefer comfortable chairs in an open room. Still others prefer their offices, so that they can sit behind their desk surrounded by the totemic icons of professional practice such as certifications and graduate degrees. Whatever gives the clients or potential clients confidence in the mediator's competence is probably correct. Check that photographs on the wall are not too controversial; a fun-house picture of the mediator shaking hands with the devil is not a terribly good idea.

Some mediators prefer to use a professional office because it indicates to clients that they are in responsible hands. The room may be located in a law firm or other organization. Some mediators have offices in their residences. A few are prepared to meet in the clients' residence, which gives them an opportunity to learn more about the family. The participants may be more comfortable in their own home, but a residence is often full of distractions such as telephones and doorbells. Also, a too-familiar setting may detract from the process; as a guest, the mediator may seem to have less authority.

Where sessions are held is, of course, a matter of judgment or necessity. Most mediators prefer that sessions take place in their own offices, but those connected with mediation centers may prefer to use the centers' offices; a mediator's image may be enhanced by the impartial reputation of such an organization.

A hotel room may be another option. Clients may not want other people to know they are having family problems. Because mediation is private, it can be provided wherever convenient to the parties. It does not have to take place in the local courthouse, which may be in an inconvenient downtown area. Many mediators establish their practices in suburban communities, convenient to the clientele they serve. Private family mediation has developed most rapidly in upscale communities, where families are able to afford the service.

Wherever the mediation takes place, the setting should contribute to a peaceful atmosphere. The decor should be carefully selected. What message does the room communicate to clients?

The furnishings should express neutral rather than controversial values; certain colors contribute to a tranquil mood.

Furniture should be comfortable and conveniently arranged. The mediator should sit in a neutral position, not where one of the parties appears to be favored. The room should be inspected to ensure that every participant will feel comfortable with the setting. Will anyone feel slighted or favored by being seated in a particular chair? Even having to face a window or being too close to a noisy air conditioner may upset a party. Mediators should do everything possible to ensure an atmosphere of impartiality.

Whether the meeting room is located in an office or a residence, the setting should be quiet, discreet, and convenient. The mediator should provide adequate parking, rest rooms, telephones and other communications equipment, and a copier. Security should be kept in mind. Mediation is facilitated when clients can set aside all other concerns except those they have come together to discuss. There will be more than enough stress without any external sources of annoyance.

The Initial Meeting

Before beginning a mediation, an initial meeting of the mediator and the clients should be scheduled so all parties know what to expect and how to proceed. The mediator should never assume that clients understand what happens in mediation. Two quite different functions take place, bargaining and collaboration. Many people don't understand what it means to collaborate, so the first order of business is to explain not just the mediator's role but the brutal reality that the parties themselves will have to work together and share in the problem solving in order to reach an agreement.

Mediators must make it clear that though they will help when possible, it is the responsibility of the parties to engage in the bargaining and problem solving. This should be pointed out at the initial meeting and then reaffirmed over and over again during the mediation.

Not every client who agrees to meet with a mediator expects to settle. Some are there because they were ordered to appear by a judge or encouraged to participate by a lawyer. They may be stalling for time. Such a party may be skeptical about the process, willing to spend a few hours with a mediator but anticipating that the lawyers will soon be back fighting in court. The mediator's ability to convince both parties to participate fully in the mediation leads to a first tenuous grasp on the case.

Early in the initial meeting, the goals of mediation should be described in general terms. At this stage the mediator should not go into the issues, but simply explain the procedure. The parties must be convinced that they will both benefit from reaching a satisfactory conclusion.

The clients are seeing the mediator for the first time, and both will be judging competence and neutrality. They have not yet signed a retainer agreement or agreed to pay; the mediator and the process are still being sold.

In presenting themselves, mediators might reflect on the environment within which family disputes arise. Clients come to the table dragging all the emotional luggage they have accumulated during their relationship. They may not be able to speak to each other without becoming angry; they may have quite different perceptions of their problem. The mediator knows nothing of these until the clients begin to talk.

As one mediator described the situation: "They are beyond logic, caught in an emotional trap. The mediator must free them, encourage them to begin thinking like adults again. But they have to see it for themselves. You can't force them to be rational."

One party may have persuaded the other to come to mediation; therefore the mediator must take care not to appear to be too close to one party lest the other experience a spasm of distrust. Either party or both may be thinking: "What my spouse wants can't be good for me." Both parties must believe that the mediator will be neutral; each may hope to make the mediator an accomplice later, but for now they need evidence of impartiality.

The first meeting, before the parties have agreed to go forward, can be delicate. Family mediation is never easy work, but the initial session may be the most difficult of all. The mediator may wonder: "Why did they choose me? What do they know about me? What do they expect of me?" New York mediator Adriane Berg may have been referring to that moment when she said, "Real mediators sweat."

As part of describing the mediation process, mediators explain their need to elicit sufficient information from the clients to identify and analyze the issues at stake. The parties should feel free to ask questions, because it is important that they understand the preliminary work that must be done before serious substantive discussions can take place.

Some mediators distribute informational pamphlets about their services; these can be mailed to clients in advance of the first meeting. The Academy of Family Mediators publishes such a pamphlet.

The clients may not know what to expect and may have been pressured into coming, but they must be persuaded to enter negotiations voluntarily and work cooperatively with each other and the mediator. They should be told they are free to leave mediation at any time, but reminded that the alternative may be expensive litigation. They should also be told that they will have to discuss their problems openly, share information, and live up to whatever obligations they assume as part of a settlement. Unless each of them believes that the other will abide by such commitments, a final resolution is unlikely. At first they may not trust each other, but that must change to reach settlement.

To be convinced of the mediator's impartiality, the parties should be involved in making procedural decisions whenever possible. Another critical factor in being impartial is gender neutrality; some family mediators prefer to work as part of a male-female team for this reason. Acting alone, a male mediator should be especially sensitive to the perceptions of female clients, and vice versa. Mediators who use sports terminology such as "level playing field" or "rules of the game," for example, may find that the phrases are commonly understood by both sexes but may alienate women. Thus the image of impartiality is tarnished, if not lost.

Mediators who have strong opinions about child care or other issues that may arise in the discussions should disclose them at the outset, not later. If one or both parties do not share these beliefs, they may decide to withdraw or the mediator may decide not to take the case. If the mediator's opinions are controversial, this is probably for the best.

Certain values should not be compromised, but a mediator should not and probably cannot impose values upon the clients. Does this mean family mediators can only work with like-minded clients? No; they can maintain their own values, but not force clients to accept them. It is a question of impartiality that must be answered depending on the case. A zealous advocate of joint custody, for example, may not care to mediate a case where the father wants nothing more to do with his child.

Mediators with rigid views on correct behavior within a family may be shocked by some of the arrangements that more liberal parents arrive at in their separation agreements. Parties that do not share certain basic philosophies with the mediator might be well advised to go elsewhere. This sometimes arises when a mediator comes from a different religion than the clients. Some faiths have strict rules about family relationships that are not compatible with some parties' desires and expectations.

Some mediators have strong views on mediation itself, and these too should be revealed at the initial conference. Isolina Ricci, a California mediator, gives her clients a one-page document that explains how she mediates. The handout describes certain ground rules she uses to guide the parties through a series of meetings. Some aspects of her approach are unique. For example, everything one party tells her she communicates to the other; she is not willing to keep secrets. Also, she will discuss the negotiations with the attorneys, calling them from time to time on her own initiative to keep them informed. Ricci is not a lawyer. She only prepares parts of separation agreements that relate to parenting rights and responsibilities, so provisions on property or support must be handled by the couple's attorneys. Such differences from normal mediation procedures should be explained in advance so the parties can decide whether they want to mediate under those conditions.

The parties should also be told how the role of mediation differs from that of other professions, such as therapy, counseling, custody evaluation, and arbitration. Mediation is not therapy, although some mediators try to improve their clients' ability to communicate or to work together in the future, which may involve some behavioral modification. It should be made perfectly clear that the mediator will not make decisions for the clients, intervene in their future lives, or file a report with any court or other government agency.

Mediators should discuss the need for clients to confide. Unless both parties are willing to share information with the mediator and each other, the mediator may not be able to help them reach a mutually agreeable settlement. Sometimes this becomes a problem. For example, one spouse may be involved in a business deal that will have an effect on future finances but involves confidential business secrets that cannot be shared, perhaps even because of some legal prohibition. What should the mediator do?

The answer depends on the particular circumstances, but the problem should be discussed with both parties so that they understand why certain information cannot be provided. Sometimes a mediator may be entrusted with information that the other party is not privy to. Not every mediator is willing to keep secrets; each must decide about that and reveal the stance to the clients.

Mediation is voluntary; either party can withdraw at any time, for any reason or no reason and without having to explain. There will be no record of the discussions, and the party who leaves owes nothing beyond what is already due the mediator for time spent on the matter. Despite all this, despite the exit door always remaining open, both parties usually stay in a mediation until the end.

Mediation may be voluntary, but that does not mean one of the parties may not have been pressured to participate. Both parties should be asked why they agreed to mediation; one may have been more reluctant than the other, and it could have an effect on the final settlement if concessions were made to persuade the reluctant party to participate. Also, a spouse who has already asked for a divorce may have conceded something, because there is a price to be paid for asking (more on this later).

Inequalities may also crop up in other kinds of family disputes. For example, in some families parents see no need to bargain with an adolescent child. The only bargaining chip some children have against their parents is assertiveness, perhaps threatening to move out of the home. Of course, if the parents would be glad to see a child leave, even that power is useless.

At the first interview, the mediator should try to discover each person's motivation for being in the mediation. Why have the parties decided to mediate? How serious are they about reaching an agreement?

If one party is reluctant to participate, the response must be to change that person's mind by encouraging both parties to negotiate in good faith—not just the reluctant one, but both: pressure on only one side places the mediator's impartiality in doubt. By making the same point to both, the mediator demonstrates a nonpartisan position. This is especially important before the retainer agreement is signed. Until then, neither party is committed to the process. Later on, when the parties have settled in, changes will take place as they sense the possibility of resolving their dispute, and that is when they begin to work together to solve whatever problems remain. At that stage the mediator can be more directive in bringing the mediation to a conclusion.

Scheduling Later Meetings

At the initial meeting, a client may ask how many sessions will be required to reach agreement. With much data still unknown, this question cannot be answered yet, but the mediator can describe the plan for subsequent meetings and work out a schedule for them.

The schedule of meetings should be convenient for both parties. Mediation belongs to them, not the mediator, and at every step they should participate in planning the procedure. Talking about the schedule provides an opportunity to encourage them to collaborate with each other, rather than expecting the mediator to decide for them. No matter how often they are told they will have to work with each other, clients still may tend to treat the mediator as an arbitrator and ask for procedural decisions; scheduling is one chance to reinforce their self-determination.

Most mediators approach scheduling pragmatically. After becoming acquainted with the parties and their problems, it may be possible to suggest some logical sequence of events. Some mediators like to begin with the least controversial aspects of the case, hoping their clients will fall into the habit of agreeing. Others like to start with the most intractable issue. This is a matter of judgment, based on sizing up the participants. Parties will usually defer to the mediator about the order in which issues are to be discussed, relying on the mediator's experience, but to encourage them to participate, the mediator should allow them to discuss that subject.

Structured mediation, discussed in depth later, affects scheduling if it is used. It breaks the subject areas into packages of issues designed to encourage the parties to collaborate in resolving their differences. By starting out with parenting issues rather than the amount of child support, the mediator encourages the parties to collaborate first before they may decide to haggle later.

In selecting topics for the initial sessions, a mediator should be careful to address each party's concerns, once again to reinforce the atmosphere of fairness. If the clients differ about where in the order of mediation an issue should be handled, the mediator should not brush the conflict aside but attempt to fashion a mutually acceptable compromise. These procedural matters do not go to the heart of the parties' controversy, but how they are resolved may set a tone for later discussions. Agreement on procedure may lead to collaboration on matters of substance later on. Mutual problem-solving can be habit-forming.

Some mediators assign reading or homework at the initial meeting, so that parties can come to the table better prepared to discuss the substantive issues. It also may be helpful for the parties to prepare budgets, financial statements, or inventories before those matters are scheduled to be discussed. This is part of fact-gathering and should be coordinated with scheduling.

Clients may have their own ideas about how many sessions will be required. Because it is a goal to have them work together, their participation in designing the schedule should be encouraged, initially and as changes become necessary during the balance of the mediation. As much as possible the mediator should be guided by the parties.

Each mediator develops certain format preferences. The first few sessions, at least, are usually scheduled to last no more than an hour or so. This allows for an efficient flow of information but does not overwhelm the parties in what may be an emotional atmosphere. After each session, they need time to recuperate and to discuss the situation with their advisers.

Some mediators prefer to schedule sessions several days apart, but this can be adjusted at the convenience of the parties. Too much pressure on them about this matter is inadvisable, but the negotiations should not drag on needlessly.

Social workers and therapists who work as mediators may prefer to fit clients into their normal schedules. This is "a matter of personal choice," one such mediator explained. "I like to work with fifty-minute blocks because I see my other clients on that basis, so it is convenient for me to schedule mediation that way. For some clients, I make an exception. When I see them in the evening or on weekends, I may schedule longer time allotments."

Family mediations are often held in the evening for the convenience of clients who work during the day. Some mediators will schedule sessions during the weekend; others like to keep regular office hours during the week. Again, this is a matter of personal choice and the expectations of clients.

Whether the sessions are limited to fifty minutes or are allowed to run longer depends ideally on client preference. With experience, mediators develop acceptable patterns for themselves; many do not devote full time to mediation and so must fit the sessions into the other demands of life.

According to one busy mediator, "It depends upon how busy I am. When I began my practice, I really didn't care. I would spend an entire evening talking with one couple. Now I don't have time for that. I maintain an appointment book and try to keep the sessions to the allotted time."

The Retainer Agreement

At about the point that the initial meeting begins to address scheduling, the mediator should discuss the terms of a retainer agreement and encourage the clients to sign it. If they wish to discuss the agreement with their lawyers, the mediator should allow it, but a good first step is to read through the document, explaining each provision so that both parties understand why it is necessary. Sometimes a client will decide not to continue, which is probably better than having the discussions break down later. In most cases, though, the parties will be willing to sign and negotiations can commence.

Virtually all retainer agreements should be in writing so they can be referred to if questions arise later; signed agreements also help with fee collection. If the mediation is informal a written retainer may not be absolutely necessary, but even then it can act as a checklist for discussing points with the clients before they begin to bargain.

Mediated negotiations cannot begin until the participants authorize a mediator to act on their behalf. The signed retainer agreement does this, and also confirms clients' relationship with each other. It provides basic guidelines for the mediation, including information exchange, confidentiality, and protection from liability, and specifies the rate, method, and allocation of payment. These and other matters need to be specified before the substantive negotiations begin. The sample retainer agreement in Exhibit 3.1 covers most of the essential points.

Exhibit 3.1. Sample Retainer Agreement.

The parties, here under, have asked _____ to serve as the sole mediator of their negotiations as to a proposed marital separation agreement. The parties agree to negotiate in good faith toward such a settlement and to provide the mediator with full and accurate information reasonably required by the mediator to understand the issues presented. The mediator may require either party to supplement such information.

It is up to the parties to negotiate the terms of their settlement agreement. The mediator does not have authority to impose a settlement upon the parties, but is being retained to help them in their negotiations. If the parties are able to reach an agreement, the mediator will record the understanding of the parties. That report shall be submitted to the parties' personal attorneys for their review and incorporation into a formal separation agreement.

The mediator has agreed to provide impartial mediation services. Mediation sessions will be scheduled at the convenience of the parties and will be private. Other persons may attend only with the permission of the parties and of the mediator. The mediator may sometimes meet privately with one of the parties, but only with the permission of the other party.

The mediator has advised the parties that they may terminate the mediation at any point, paying the mediator only for whatever time and expenses have accrued to that time. The mediator in turn reserves the right to withdraw from the case at the mediator's discretion if it seems appropriate or if a reasonable agreement between the parties seems unlikely.

The mediator has advised the parties that questions may arise concerning their respective legal rights during the course of negotiations. To protect such rights each party has been encouraged to seek advice from legal counsel. There is no limitation on the right to seek professional advice at any time during the mediation.

Confidential information disclosed by the parties during this mediation will not be divulged by the mediator. All records, reports, or other documents received by the mediator while serving in that capacity shall be confidential. The mediator shall not be compelled to divulge such information or testify in regard to the mediation on behalf of either party in any adversary proceeding or judicial forum. The mediator urges the parties, on their part, to keep such information confidential so that there can be a full and candid exchange.

Each party agrees, during the course of the mediation, to respect the privacy of the other and not to transfer disputed property or to assume additional debts without mutual consent. Any interim agreements between the parties will be discussed with the mediator before being entered into.

The parties agree not to hold the mediator liable or to include the mediator in any judicial proceedings as to this mediation or as to the parties' relationship. The mediator will not participate on behalf of either party in any subsequent proceeding.

The mediator's fees will be $_____ per hour, plus any reasonable expenses incurred. The parties will be billed periodically for the outstanding amount, for which they agree to be jointly liable.

Party _____   Party _____
Mediator _____   Date _____

Mediators may want to delete or add provisions to their retainer agreements as they develop their practices. If child custody or visitation issues will be involved in the mediation, an additional provision can be added to the retainer agreement along these lines: "In connection with discussing the best interests of a child, the mediator may interview the child privately to determine the child's attitude about custodial arrangements, but only with the permission of both parties. With their approval, the mediator may also obtain a professional opinion as to the best interests of the child. That opinion will be shared with both parties and the cost shared equally between them."

Some parties may not want a mediator to meet privately with their child. If so, the mediator needs to know in advance, and a clause such as the example above should bring that information out. (For that matter, some mediators do not think it necessary or helpful to meet with children, a viewpoint covered in more detail later.)

If the mediator is a mental health professional, an outside opinion as to the children may not be necessary. In any case, parties should not be forced to pay for such an opinion unless they believe it would be helpful.

Once a retainer agreement has been signed and a proposed structure of the mediation discussed, mediators may give the clients a schedule or chart of events that follow, indicating the flow from one package of issues to another. Worksheets or forms may be distributed, depending on the kinds of issues that will be considered. Some mediators assign homework. In this new and growing field, various approaches have been adopted and others are being created.

The Early Sessions

Family mediators do more than convene meetings with clients and allow them to talk. They intervene to persuade them to participate and to reach agreement. Clients need to see progress. Getting them

to agree on minor issues sometimes paves the way for major concessions later. Success breeds success. When both parties begin to
work towards agreement, their negotiations will gain momentum
and become increasingly productive.

Experienced mediators use a variety of techniques to get clients
involved. Initially they have to appraise each party's ability to
engage in negotiations. The parties seldom have equal power.
Before the bargaining can begin, a mediator should attempt to
establish equilibrium, perhaps suggesting a more assertive approach
to a passive individual. This requires great care; the mediator
should never appear to favor or speak for an apparently weaker
party.

Unless both parties are reasonably well prepared, discussions
may not be successful. Reluctance to make concessions is not the
issue; that can be resolved. In the words of one experienced mediator: "In dozens of cases I have seen reluctant parties change their
attitude during the negotiations, particularly when I caucus with
them in private and they let their hair down. The possibility that
they will not be able to settle becomes a challenge. Sometimes I am
shocked at how far they are willing to go to reach closure."

But equalizing the parties' ability to negotiate is another matter. It is not enough to say that a mediator should not favor either
party by trying to achieve a balance between them. That formula
is helpful, but does not specify what a mediator needs to do to
achieve a balance.

Some participants need coaching before they are ready to negotiate. No two people have equal bargaining ability. One or both
clients may need time to prepare; one may need more help than
the other. The inequality may be so gross that bargaining would be
improper. People who are incapable of handling their own affairs
need someone else to represent their interests, in which case family mediation may or may not be appropriate and the mediator
must say so.

Under any circumstances the mediator needs to ask a few tough
questions of the clients before they confront each other at the

negotiating table: Have you analyzed the situation? Have you identified your goals? Are you ready to confront each other? Have you thought about the interests of children and other important people not in the room today? If either party cannot answer all these questions in the affirmative, more thought or homework is necessary before proceeding.

When the Discussions Begin

Even proper preparation by the clients may not prevent a shouting match as they start to discuss the issues. They may say they are sick of bickering, but bad habits die hard, so they continue to snarl. But the mediator must control the climate of the discussions and persuade them to adopt a productive approach. Some techniques for lowering the decibels are well known, such as simply sitting quietly until the shouting dies down, but it may be more effective to explain that nothing more can be done until both sides control themselves. Or the mediator can call a recess or turn to a less emotional subject.

Crying or otherwise losing control of emotions is fairly common early in the mediation process. Tears may indicate that a person is grieving about the death of the marriage, or may be a submissive way to express anger or a technique that worked to extract concessions in the past. The ability to interpret emotional displays, which are methods of self-expression, is an important skill for mediators.

Some couples have forgotten how to communicate with each other; they talk but don't hear. One spouse may complain that the other no longer listens, and the other may respond that the first simply makes no attempt to understand. The same is true of other family relationships. Adults may say that they have become invisible to their children, and the children complain that their parents don't listen to what they are trying to tell them.

Mediators must determine whether parties are getting through to each other. Their probing might begin: "What I think I'm hearing you say is . . ." The response will likely be telling. Sometimes couples stop listening to each other when a particular subject has become too painful to discuss. Still, a skilled mediator can reopen channels of communication that have not been used for years.

One of the parties may need to hear an apology, and that can be a sticking point. An individual may be unwilling to negotiate until certain feelings are recognized through an apology that acknowledges a mistake, asks forgiveness, or explains. It must be done correctly. The mediator can set the stage by asking, "What can your spouse say that would help?"

If the response indicates that an apology would help, the mediator can coach the other party to say something like, "I'm sorry that what I did hurt you. Will you forgive me?" Of course, such an apology must be sincere and deserving of forgiveness. This may be made easier because mediation discussions are confidential and there is little risk that an apology in such circumstances will be used as an admission in court. At any rate, apologies may oil the gears of negotiation. An apology should be acknowledged, by the mediator if not by the injured party.

Apology is an example of what may go on in early discussions between the parties. Of such early discussions, one mediator said: "I always listen carefully, particularly at the initial meeting. When I hear something that one of the parties is not responding to, I spell it out. I try to dig under the surface, asking questions and explaining. Sometimes, even the most obvious points are not being heard. I make certain that they are."

Members of a family do not necessarily listen to each other. The mediator may have to identify and translate whatever is blocking their ability to understand each other. Do certain words carry different meanings to the other individual? Are their values in conflict? It is quite normal for people to screen out views they can't accept.

"It can be very frustrating," said one mediator. "They are speaking the same language, but they are not exchanging information. Strange, when you realize that they have been sharing a marriage.

Sometimes I suspect that they are using some secret code that no one else can understand, but then I discover that they are not hearing it either. I have to make them use words that all three of us can understand."

Questions and more questions are what lubricates the mediation process, clarifying what the parties are trying to say to each other, bringing their desires and emotions and preferences to the surface so that they can be considered and resolved. Alan C. Tidwell's 1994 article on the subject, "Not Effective Communication but Effective Persuasion," points out that the important question in mediation is whether the parties can persuade each other to make changes in their initial positions. Parties need help in expressing themselves and may be handicapped by negative attitudes toward dispute resolution that they may have adopted in the past, based on personal experiences (Tidwell, 1994, p. 8). Mediators can restructure the parties' statements and expand the informational resources available to them. Tidwell believes that mediation is a communications process, and that the extent to which it succeeds depends upon the mediator's ability to persuade and the parties' willingness to be persuaded.

The Caucus

Parties can't reach agreement without confronting each other, but important changes can take place in separate sessions called caucuses, during which the mediator obtains confidential information and discusses the needs, desires, attitudes, and positions of each party.

The Academy of Family Mediators cautions mediators about caucuses, particularly about whether information obtained in them should be confidential. The academy holds that private caucuses between the mediator and one party are acceptable if both parties agree to it in advance, and that both must also agree in advance on the question of confidentiality: Should the mediator withhold information learned in caucus from the other party?

Mediators may also desire to have separate meetings with other people who are not directly involved in the mediation but whose views or knowledge may help. Strictly speaking these are not caucuses, but they also require prior approval by the parties.

Some family mediators do not take advantage of caucuses or meetings with outside people for fear of jeopardizing the appearance of impartiality. One party may become suspicious if the mediator suggests a meeting with the other. Usually mediators will not schedule caucuses until they are confident that they have earned the trust of both parties. But when that has happened, and when the joint discussions have bogged down, separate meetings where parties can be more candid about their needs and expectations may help. More joint sessions at such points may only force the parties into fixed positions from which retreat is increasingly difficult.

When a party refuses to budge, a mediator can use a caucus to explore specific areas of accommodation and to explain that further concessions may be necessary. A caucus also may help when parties are having trouble communicating with each other. They may say things to the mediator alone that they are unwilling to express to each other.

Before suggesting caucuses, the mediator should decide which party to meet with first. Alternating between the two helps avoid the appearance of pressuring one more than the other. Joint meetings should continue when appropriate, but through caucuses a mediator may gain a better understanding of the parties' willingness to compromise. By identifying possible trade-offs or mutual concessions, a mediator may be able to facilitate settlement.

In the field of labor relations, where professional negotiators are involved, much productive mediation takes place away from the primary negotiating table, often during caucuses. But in family mediation, where the parties tend to be less sophisticated, most discussions should take place in joint sessions. The emphasis should be on the parties talking directly to each other, not communicating through the mediator, and the focus should be on self-determination, with the parties trying to persuade each other. The family mediator should be a facilitator, not a manipulator. In labor relations, the caucus is king; collective bargaining is carried out between organizations. Although formal negotiations take place at the table, much of the mediator's effective work is done with smaller groups that represent various union factions or levels of management. Not so in family mediation.

The Nine-Step Format

When clients are prepared to talk substantively, the work can begin. The following nine procedural steps are recommended.

Step One: Making Interim Arrangements

Initial agreements may have to be worked out with the clients to provide child care or support while the negotiations are being carried out, or to persuade one to move out of the home. The mediator may have to suggest some interim regime to deal with these immediate problems. Even at this early stage, the mediator may have to be somewhat directive here, but should be evenhanded to the extent possible.

Interim arrangements should be understood not to prejudice the final outcome of the negotiations, but this can be problematic; for example, a spouse may not be willing to leave home for fear of losing bargaining position. In such a case the mediator may suggest other arrangements. These preliminary matters can be difficult because the mediator most likely does not yet know the clients well enough to anticipate whether they will make concessions about such things.

Step Two: Getting Clients to Talk

The mediator must learn about the clients. Giving them an opportunity to tell their stories helps to assemble information and to define their relationship and their respective needs, desires, and perceptions. During this early sharing of information and feelings, the mediator must make certain each participant is understood by the other, not because it will lead to immediate settlement but because it will clarify the issues between them. Some statements may eliminate misunderstandings, others may widen the breach; in any case, each side will hear the other describe what has gone wrong and what that person seeks from the negotiations. By explaining to the mediator, they will be clarifying the issues to each other. Thus these discussions should take place with both parties present.

Sometimes one party will claim that the other already knows the first party's feelings about a subject. The mediator should not accept this and should ask for an explanation for the mediator's own benefit. People often assume their spouses understand their positions when it is not so; marriage does not confer the ability to read minds. The needs, desires, and perceptions of each party must be verbalized so that differences can come to the surface.

The mediator should take notes. These can be reviewed to refresh the memory and prepare for subsequent sessions, when the parties' positions may have shifted. The clients should be assured, however, that the notes are solely for the mediator's use and will not be made available to anyone else. Indeed, the mediator is obliged to maintain confidentiality in the storage and disposal of any such records; if they are later used as the basis for research or training, the obligation still stands and the information must be rendered anonymous.

Some mediators prepare a memorandum for the parties at the end of each session, describing what issues have been resolved and what still needs to be done. This should be carefully edited to eliminate confidential material or anything else that might harm the negotiations.

Step Three: Identifying Areas of Agreement

The parties may have already agreed on some aspects of their separation. It is useful to identify these areas, not only to demonstrate that agreement between them is possible but to confirm that certain matters are no longer in dispute. What they have already done gives them a vested interest in reaching a final settlement; if they are unable to agree on the remaining issues, the benefit of earlier agreements may be lost. The parties are walking together toward a settlement. One step leads to another.

Step Four: Clarifying the Issues

The remaining issues between the parties should be clearly defined, and this is where clients particularly need the mediator's help. They may disagree on certain facts, but their primary problem is the divergence of needs, desires, and expectations. They must express themselves; the mediator must clarify what they are trying to say to each other. They must define the issues; the mediator must restate their explanations until it is certain each party understands what the other is trying to say. The mediator must eliminate misunderstandings but also elicit additional information both sides can use to design a formula for settlement. The parties may have to be encouraged to consider additional dimensions of their problem to ensure that the eventual settlement is realistic.

The mediator must ask questions that are intrusive without offending the parties. Unfortunately, emotions may be slumbering under the surface of a discussion like land mines. Things may be moving forward in perfect harmony until someone mentions Fido, and then the room explodes. Seemingly valueless personal property can block resolution if one party is overwhelmingly attached to it emotionally.

When unresolved issues are identified they become the focus of the mediation, so the parties must agree that these are the areas they must work on. Then the mediator can discuss how each subject should be handled, helping the parties prioritize their concerns and deciding with them which issues are of greater or lesser importance and how to proceed based on that ranking.

Step Five: Obtaining Information

Before the parties can hammer out an agreement, they will have to share all relevant and material information. For the mediator to know enough to assist in the process, they have to make extensive disclosures, including financial information. The Academy of Family Mediators tells mediators to "require disclosure of all relevant information . . . as would reasonably occur in the judicial discovery process" (Academy of Family Mediators Standards of Practice, 1995, VI[H]).

This requirement may overshoot the mark. The kind of discovery required for a court trial has become a notorious burden because an attorney can request any documents or depositions that are claimed relevant and material to the case. A deposition involves the examination under oath of a potential witness by the other party's attorney. In court, a judge may be asked to rule on the extent of discovery. If all this were required in mediation, the process would become unworkable. The attorneys for the parties would be making demands for documents and depositions, arguing motions, and requiring the mediator to rule on evidentiary questions.

Judicial discovery rules have no place in mediation. A mediation session is not a hearing but an informal opportunity to discuss problems. Disclosure in mediation should be more limited. The obligation should be to disclose whatever information is reasonably relevant and material, leaving it to the parties and the mediator to draw the line.

If one party refuses to make proper disclosure, the other has several options: carry out an independent investigation, draw adverse conclusions from the refusal, or refuse to mediate. A mediator should not be expected to rule on procedural questions, but should rely on persuasion, explaining to the reluctant party that a court may mandate disclosure; if failure to disclose in mediation means no settlement can be reached, the other party's lawyer probably will dig out the necessary information later anyway. Usually this argument will elicit the information.

A mediator can ask both parties to submit financial statements that disclose all their assets and liabilities. This information needs to be shared; financial reality is more likely to lead to a realistic settlement. "You can't get blood from a turnip" isn't just a saying, it's the truth. With a clear picture of what is available, the parties can design a sensible arrangement for their future.

The differences between people may have more to do with emotions than dollars. Nevertheless, better informed and more reliable settlements are produced when both parties are aware of the realities of their situation. The mediator must clear away any obstacles to communication and maximize the parties' exploration of alternatives. This can best be done when all relevant facts are placed on the table.

At some point a party may say that something is none of the mediator's business, so the mediator must be prepared to explain why the information is relevant to the negotiations. How much information is sufficient may be debatable, but it would not be proper for one of the parties to hide property or sources of income from the other. On the other hand, it is unrealistic to believe that every card will be turned face up on the table; the mediator must decide how extensive disclosure needs to be and then convince reluctant parties to comply.

Concealed assets or a secret plan for the future can harm the mediation, but as the mediator learns more about the case, some or all of this information may surface. As one experienced mediator puts it, "Don't be afraid to ask questions. One thing will lead to another. Be alert. Listen carefully. [Parties] may not be lying, but they may not be volunteering all of the information either. You have to dig it out." These questions should focus on the parties' history and current situation.

In complicated cases more than one session may be required to develop detailed information, particularly about assets, expenses, and financial expectations. Both parties should be present during this process, even though one or both may feel it is merely a tedious exploration of irrelevancies. "Let's get on with it," one of them may say. "We're ready to settle. There's no need for these details." But usually the parties should be persuaded to continue digging. By asking intelligent questions that raise issues they may not have thought about, the mediator can often demonstrate the need for further investigation. As Newt Gingrich says of his congressional style of conciliation: "Listen, learn, help, lead."

Mediators should ask themselves additional questions during the entire interrogation: Which areas do the parties seem hesitant to discuss? Why are they avoiding certain subjects? Are they relevant to the underlying issues? This can reveal a critical sticking point between the parties. There may have been an unpleasant incident neither client wants to talk about but which blocks negotiations. Perhaps one spouse caught the other in an act of adultery; neither may want to talk about it, but they may have to deal with it before they can move ahead. Such an incident certainly affects their attitudes toward each other. Any number of concerns may be involved; perhaps an apology is called for. And the mediator must be privy to such secrets to understand their relationship.

Sometimes the motivation to settle needs to ripen, and the mediator should recognize when the parties need more time to consider their options. They will be talking to many outsiders about their problems—relatives, friends, business associates, various professional advisers. Rarely do discussions in mediation go untalked about afterwards. The parties will not only seek outside advice, but opinions will be thrust upon them from their attorneys, their hairdressers, and who knows who else.

One party may need more time between meetings than the other, perhaps because of a business trip or to take a vacation. Then the negotiations may have to be suspended. This is normal and can be worked around, but sometimes the mediator should encourage the clients to meet more frequently. For example, when the couple's children are away on summer vacation, frequent or even full-time negotiations may be possible. Outside events can be used to press for settlement.

A mediator must justify the time spent on fact-finding by convincing the parties that the information sought is relevant and material. Otherwise, they will become impatient with the process.

Step Six: Negotiating

The heart of family mediation is bargaining and collaboration. To reach settlement, the parties must exchange promises. They can be assisted but must evolve their own solutions to the issues.

Maintaining a productive dialogue is essential. A mediator does this by getting the parties to abandon negative habits such as blaming each other, which may destroy whatever liking may still exist between them, by guiding them away from an overly adversarial attitude.

Thus the successful mediator is part salesperson, part translator, part teacher, part broker, part psychologist, part family counselor, part chameleon, part dramatist, part manipulator, part trickster, part public servant. All those roles and more serve as a bridge between a negative relationship and a working partnership. An effective mediator is as much artist as technician.

Clients are usually quite prepared to prove that the other party is totally wrong and that they are perfectly right. Playing such games, however, prevents the commencement of problem solving. But when they realize they have to deal with each other, they can begin to make progress. At that stage, they may indicate that they are prepared to make a deal, to begin to bargain.

Family mediation is unique in that some issues are adversarial and lend themselves to bargaining, but others involve mutual interests where the parties should collaborate. Dividing the family silver may be only a matter of bargaining to swap a fork for a spoon, but selecting a summer camp for a child is best a collaborative effort that reflects a mutual concern for the child. A mediator should help the parties understand the difference between the two techniques and lead them to use the right one for each issue.

Bargaining requires a willingness to compromise. Sometimes this involves making bids and counterbids. The mediator may have to fish for the first bid, then the second. At the outset neither party may be willing to make a move, but as they continue to bargain they usually become committed to the success of the process and settlement becomes a goal.

One excellent mediator expressed it this way: "Perhaps it is a chemical reaction, deeply implanted in the human psyche. I have seen it happen time and time again. The parties will start out almost unable to stay in the same room together. Several sessions later, they are dealing with each other like old cronies at a weekly poker game. Is it addictive? Is there something in human nature that makes them want to make deals? Don't ask me to explain it, but I know that my reputation as a mediator is based on that phenomenon." He wasn't talking about family mediation on this occasion, but it still applies.

Certain elements influence bargaining: need fulfillment, expectation level, influence, knowledge, status, self-confidence, and personality. Keeping those elements in mind, a family mediator can guide clients through the process.

The parties will determine the bargaining pace. The mediator must realize that some parties find it stressful to give up the intimacies of their relationship, whether it be the emotions of marriage or the dependencies of childhood. Those transformations require people to work their way through complex feelings about the past. It is not unusual for the emotions that accompany such changes to make an appearance in the early stages of a mediation. The mediator should be prepared for displays of anger and sadness, for shouting and tears.

One party may accuse the mediator of favoring the other on an issue, but a mediator should refuse to be drawn into arguments and should just point out that the mediator and the issue at hand are two different things. Of course, the mediator who has indeed been unfair must acknowledge the mistake and move on. Mediators do make mistakes, and are permitted to do so; but they must keep discussions focused on their clients' problems rather than on their own faults.

Parties who want to bargain should be encouraged. They may have their own ideas about which issues should be addressed first, and this is also fine. However, they should take their time. A mediator should not try to push them into quick settlement. At the outset of bargaining, some people are particularly vulnerable because they don't know how to do it; others are inflexible because they have adopted a particular way of relating to situations that makes it difficult for them to consider more effective ways. A person who has been dominated by others, for example, may no longer be in the habit of making demands and may grab the first offer that comes along even if it is clearly inadequate. Such a person should at least be cautioned that better offers may come.

There may be extenuating circumstances. In one case a detective hired by a husband found the client's wife in bed with her lover. Playing on her feelings of guilt, the husband persuaded the woman to give up the family home, most of their marital property, and custody of their two children, and to accept from him only a small stipend for the first year of their separation. A court overturned that contract on the basis that it was coercive. If a mediator had been involved in the negotiations, the situation might have turned out differently. At the least, she probably would have been encouraged to hire an attorney.

It can work both ways. A husband, caught flagrante delicto and overwhelmed by guilt, might agree to pay more than he can afford. Later, unable to meet his obligations, he might default, leaving his spouse with even less money than she would have obtained from a more reasonable settlement. A mediator would likely encourage the parties to discuss the practicality of such a settlement before it became finalized.

A mediator may decide that a realistic settlement is impossible. One couple that came to mediation had four teenage children. He earned a modest salary as an accountant; she had never held an outside job. When they decided to divorce and talked to a mediator, he quickly saw that the husband's salary was not enough to support the separated family. The wife needed a job. The mediator suggested that she take up bookkeeping. During job training, her personality changed; the couple continued to live together, but she became more independent. By this time the husband wanted to stay married, but she had developed her own life, wanted to leave him, and found a job. Only at that point could the mediator help the couple reach a settlement that made it possible for them to divorce.

Some mediators believe that the major roadblock to settlement is a lack of information, and that when the parties are able to agree on the facts their disagreements will inevitably be resolved. But others think emotions and the conflicting perceptions the parties bring to the table are more influential than the facts. The truth probably lies somewhere in between. A settlement may depend partially upon factual clarification and partially on a convergence in the parties' attitudes.

People are motivated by a desire for fulfillment. Their needs and desires provide insight into the dispute resolution process. Each party wants something from the other; only the mutual satisfaction of such desires makes a solution possible. When the parties understand each other's needs, their positions will usually converge.

Family mediations are rarely zero-sum games where the only issues that matter are ones of distribution, a dollar more for one spouse here and a dollar less for the other spouse there. Usually some interests are mutual, and the mediator fosters the clients' discovery of that fact. The mutuality of some interests is obvious: bringing up the children, for example. Few parents would argue that one should get to decide on the kids' religious training in exchange for the other being allowed to raise them as vegetarians. Such decisions will normally be made mutually, not on a distributive basis.

Other issues such as the level of family support or the allocation of property may involve bargaining, but even there, common interests may intrude. Not many parties want to destroy their former spouse. More frequently a community of interest will survive, diluting the hostility of negotiations. Collaboration is the ideal. The mediator wants the parties to collaborate if possible, bargain if not.

When parties bargain, those with high aspirations tend to do better. Each party brings some level of expectation to the table and is prepared to accept some level of risk. Their behavior tends to depend on their anticipation of success and their evaluation of the potential risks and rewards. If one party comes to the negotiations with higher expectations than the other, that party is likely to do better. That is a fact. Negotiators who have low expectations on distributive issues tend to be satisfied with less, whether the bargaining is part of family mediation or of some other negotiating process.

It is in bargaining negotiations rather than those involving mutual interests where a spouse without business experience may be willing to trade away monetary value for principle or to accept an inadequate offer. Does a mediator have the responsibility to keep that from happening? The Academy of Family Mediators has taken a realistic stance: decision-making authority rests with the parties. It is enough that the settlement be "informed and voluntary." On the other hand, some mediators will not give their blessing to a settlement that is "inadequate." But if the parties reach agreement, can abide by it, and can get it confirmed in court if necessary, they don't need the approval of the mediator. The settlement is theirs. They can do whatever they choose.

To the extent that parties bargain, mediation creates a kind of marketplace where demands and offers are made and then accepted or rejected. The mediator can assist in such negotiations but cannot stop a participant from making a "bad" bargain nor tell the parties what kind of bargains they are allowed to enter into. Either may make a mistake in bargaining, which is why mediators should encourage collaboration on issues that can be resolved that way. As noted, the interests of children usually warrant collaboration, but even on this the decision is for the parties to make. They have a right to make mistakes. Their ultimate protection is their own judgment.

Parties adjust their expectations during negotiations. They change bargaining positions as they discuss the issues and attempt to influence each other over them. Every demand or concession, every new material fact or argument is likely to reduce or increase their respective expectations. Skillful negotiators try to create doubt in an adversary's mind. Their objective is to lower that person's level of expectation without forcing an impasse. Some mediators play the same game, chipping away at the parties' positions by creating doubts and encouraging them to compromise. The parties are attempting to influence each other, probing for concessions, trying to convince the other party to settle. At the same time, the mediator may be encouraging both of them to settle.

Each party may try to persuade the mediator to put pressure on the other. The mediator must therefore take care not to become an advocate but to continue encouraging them to settle, listening to them, and from time to time clarifying what they say to be certain both sides understand.

The outcome of bargaining often depends upon relative power. Negotiating power has to do with the ability to influence the behavior of an adversary. When preparing for sessions, a mediator should evaluate the power equation, a difficult task because power is relative and always shifting.

Negotiating power can be real or apparent. The ability to force someone to do something is real power, but it is effective only to the extent that it is accepted by an adversary. Otherwise it is only potential and ineffectual. Power can't exist in a vacuum.

Influence is a form of power, though difficult to measure. The power of legitimacy is questionable. Commitment to a concept or to an ideal can be a source of power, but it can also be a weakness; people sometimes accept conventional rules without questioning their applicability. The law has force because of its legitimacy, but wanting to appear consistently law-abiding can be a weakness. In business, some individuals have become wealthy by flouting their contractual obligations; they sign contracts but only comply with them when brought to court.

A reputation for being irrational can be an asset. The bargaining table seldom rewards the weak or the timid. Unpleasant, demanding people may be excellent negotiators. In a zero-sum game, it may be profitable to bluff, and in family mediation some clients try it. Is that appropriate? Should the mediator try to convince them to stop, or simply share a visible bluff with the other party?

Knowledge can be another source of power. The more someone knows about an adversary's needs and objectives, the stronger that party may be in negotiations, though not always. After all, a person willing to take risks and tolerate uncertainty may also exert power, as may someone who is willing to ignore risk. Even in a rational world the madman may be king. The mediator should not assume clients will abide by rational guidelines. In any case, what appears rational to the mediator may not to someone else. Even mediators are captives of their cultural norms, and these should not be imposed on the clients.

Status may also influence negotiating power. A wage earner may have a psychological advantage over a member of the family who is not. Whether the dispute is between a working spouse and a nonworking mate or between a parent and child, unequal status may skew the power relationship. On the other hand, personality differences may compensate for differences in status.

A party who is constrained by time may lose bargaining power to a more patient negotiator. If an adversary can be persuaded to accept a time limit, the pressure is on. If a wage-earning spouse knows that the nonworking other has fallen in love with someone new and wants to marry again, it creates a sort of time constraint of desire, and the hastier, less generous settlement that may result reflects it.

The ability to plan, set priorities, anticipate actions, and develop a bargaining strategy can also lend power to a negotiator.

All these facets of bargaining power apply to family mediation, and the mediator should caution clients about them. A spouse is not a customer, so arms-length bargaining may not be appropriate between them. And given that negotiating within a family framework is rife with mutual interests, collaboration rather than bargaining is preferable in dealing with many issues. Even after divorcing, a couple is led by their separation into an ongoing partnership that is less intimate than marriage but not one that either will want to besmirch with fraud. Within the matrix of their future lives, the settlement will cling to their reputations. That is a strong argument for collaboration.

Still, parties should not lower their expectations to encourage collaboration. Some concessions may eventually be necessary to reach agreement, but caving in up front is not one of them. However, this is their responsibility, not the mediator's, whose primary obligation is to get them to settle.

A mediator may have to challenge clients' assumptions, usually by asking them questions such as: Are your expectations realistic? Can your demands be justified? Sometimes a mediator must confront clients with the facts, which may mean bringing new information up for discussion or telling how similar cases were decided in court. Any challenge to a client's opinion can cause a shift in priorities, so laying the facts on the table and stressing the consequences of not facing up to reality may urge them toward settlement.

It is never easy for people to admit that they are wrong or to make concessions. There is plenty of stress in family mediation, and emotions may rise so high that further discussions are impossible. Adjournment until emotional balance has been regained is then necessary. Constantly overwrought parties may need referral to therapy. Some family mediators are also therapists, but the line between the professions should be maintained. It is not appropriate for a mediator to take responsibility for a party's mental health, nor for a therapist to mediate for a patient.

As the mediator ascertains the fundamental needs, desires, and expectations of each party, and as each party understands those of the other, the dimensions of an eventual solution may begin to form in the mediator's mind and the positions of the parties may begin to converge. Gradually the discussion will evolve toward what can be done to achieve settlement.

If the parties continue to collaborate on issues, progress can continue in joint sessions. Later, caucuses may help resolve other issues that one party is not willing to discuss directly with the other. At a private meeting, the mediator can strive for additional concessions.

Sometimes a mediator uses caucuses to initiate movement. Armed with a concession from one of the parties, the mediator can try to convince the other to reciprocate. Once positions begin to converge, the mediator tries to narrow the gap, moving both toward agreement. In a series of caucuses, the major issues may diminish and later dissolve. Perhaps the mediator even obtains the commitments from each party needed to settle the case, but they were given in confidence, in caucus. How can they be brought to the surface?

Here is what one mediator does: "Later on, when I bring the parties together again, I may know that I have a settlement, but I must be certain that they will stick with what they have been telling me in private. That is when mediating becomes dicey. Either I can offer the package as my idea or present it as a hypothetical solution. Neither party wants to be the first to confirm a concession. I make it look like a simultaneous exchange."

As settlement comes near, a mediator must look for trade-offs: If the husband will pay more support per month, the wife will let him keep the car. If Grandmother can stay at her daughter's house in October, her son's family will take her for the rest of the year. A mediator has to identify areas where compromise is possible. Using these, the mediator tries to devise a formula for settlement. Sometimes that takes creativity.

"A mediator can be innovative, but only after taking the trouble to study the situation in depth." The mediator who said that explains that he always jots down alternatives, examining the pros and cons, calculating the costs, and outlining the arguments that must be made: "When I hit upon a possible solution, I go all out to sell it to the parties. I usually succeed."

Only the clients can decide what is best for them. It is their dispute and their settlement, and mediators should not try to thrust other value systems on them. Sometimes a mediator may wonder why a party is willing to accept a seemingly inadequate offer, but standing in the way of a settlement satisfactory to both clients is rarely wise. Such demurral requires humility and the understanding that a mediation is not an arbitrator, not a judge, and certainly not a god.

The mediator may have to act, however, if negotiations break down because progress toward settlement is too slow. Something must energize the process. Success can be an incentive to speed up, so the parties should leave each session with some sense of accomplishment and a clear idea of what they must do to reach the next goal. The mediator may give them homework, ask them to study a particular problem, or tell them to come back to the next session ready to resolve a certain issue. Mediation is traffic management that keeps negotiations rolling down the track.

As settlement nears, too much time between meetings is inadvisable. A client may fall under the spell of a settlement-killer, perhaps a hungry lawyer who promises better results in court or a relative who doesn't think the deal sounds too good so far. Rare is the client who prefers not to discuss the case except when the mediator is present. People like to talk about their problems, particularly when they are involved in something as exciting as a mediation. Between one session and another, clients will often acquire new attitudes and concerns. Keeping the intervals between meetings short is one way to lessen these bumps on the road to settlement.

The techniques mediators use to persuade the parties to converge are crucial to the process. In subtle ways, everything that precedes convergence should contribute to the parties' willingness to settle, particularly whatever persuaded them to collaborate or at least to negotiate effectively and without rancor. In learning to work together during the early stages, the participants should have learned that it is possible for them to hold divergent values while still collaborating to reach agreement on issues where their respective needs, desires, and interests are in harmony. Step by step, the process of mediation should make it possible for them to agree without having to give up individual values. They don't have to be friends to reach agreement. They don't even have to like each other.

Now convergence is near. Perhaps the clients have agreed on everything but the amount of child support, on which issue they are $30,000 apart. They are stuck. What can be done to prevent the last gap in agreement from creating an impasse? The mediator has to find some way to bridge that gap. First is to warn the parties that this may be their last opportunity to settle, short of going to court. But if that doesn't persuade them to continue, they may ask the mediator for ideas.

The mediator certainly may suggest splitting the difference, or adjusting other payments to compensate for the extra child support. But this is dangerous ground. Any solution the mediator offers may upset the strategy of one party who has been waiting for some final concession from the other.

Prudent mediators make proposals at caucuses. If an idea is not acceptable to one of the parties, there is no need to mention it to the other. If the suggestion seems agreeable to both, the mediator still has to figure out how to surface it at a joint session so that it becomes mutually acceptable. The need to confirm those kinds of informal agreements can arise at several stages of the mediation.

A party may express a willingness to make a certain concession during a caucus but then renege when the question comes up at a joint session. A mediator can't force a party to follow the script, but can usually obtain a promise during the caucus that the party will act in good faith, pointing out that once such a commitment has been made it is essential to honor it. Trust between each party and the mediator is important, in part as a basis for complying with commitments made in a caucus.

Step Seven: Concluding a Settlement

If the negotiations are successful, the parties reach agreement. The checklist of issues prepared earlier helps determine whether every issue has been resolved. With the clients, the mediator should then go over all the agreements in order, making sure that everyone understands what has been decided. If they do, a memorandum can be drawn up confirming the agreement. Some mediators like to do that at once, while the parties are still present, and have each of them initial the rough draft.

If closure is very near but not quite in place, the clients may ask how to close the gap. As mentioned above, this is dangerous ground and the mediator must be certain both parties actually will welcome suggestions. Timing is everything. Too early in the game, suggesting solutions can cast doubt on the mediator's impartiality. Even later it can be risky, but when the parties are facing an impasse, they may actually ask the mediator to decide for them. In general, such requests should be discouraged or denied. A mediator should leave matters of substance to the parties themselves.

On the other hand, if the parties simply can't close the gap there is little point to adding more to the cost of mediation by pro-longing the discussions. Rather than sending the parties away, the mediator might suggest an "impasse-busting" device such as MEDALOA (described in Chapter One), arbitration, or even flip-ping a coin. Depending on the importance of the remaining issues, one of these might be acceptable.

Parties have to make hard choices as they approach the end of their negotiations. They should be asked if making a few further concessions is better than reaching an impasse. They have already invested time in the mediation; this may be their final chance to settle the dispute. They have been warned what may occur if they are unable to agree, have spent time and money on mediation, and have already made substantial concessions. The parties are now under the greatest pressure to settle. It is worthwhile for the medi-ator to take advantage of their prior actions, and even of their exhaustion, to urge them once more to make one final effort to set-tle their dispute.

Suggestions from the mediator may be acceptable, but they should not come as a surprise. If a proposal has not been discussed in advance, preferably in caucuses, this is not the right time to spring it. The mediator should not try to be a last-second hero with an innovative new answer; far better for the parties to believe they invented the solution, and the way to do that is to convince them to continue negotiating.

If the parties are still unable to agree, the situation might be explained to them this way: "As long as you stick to your present positions, no agreement is possible. There will be no point holding any further meetings. But there are ways to deal with an impasse. For example, you can authorize someone else to decide the issues for you. Would you like me to suggest some ways this can be done?"

When it comes to closing a final gap, MEDALOA may be most appropriate, particularly for monetary issues. MEDALOA combines the advantages of final bargaining and last-offer arbitration, limiting the decision maker to selecting the last offer of one party or the other, nothing in between. This may serve to encourage the parties to continue bargaining, because neither will want the arbitrator to select the other's last offer. Or when they submit their last offers, the parties may work hard to narrow the gap so their offer will appear the best choice.

If the clients ask the mediator to serve as the MEDALOA arbitrator, there may be no need for a further hearing, as the mediator already knows the issues. But one or both of the parties may prefer that some other person be chosen to arbitrate, which is fine. In most cases parties will ask their mediator to serve.

Binding arbitration is also an option. O. J. Coogler favored arbitration when mediation didn't work. After his own expensive and traumatic divorce, he became convinced that there had to be a better way to resolve marital dissolution than going to court, a more rational, more civilized way of arranging a separation and divorce.

Coogler was influenced by his exposure to transactional analysis, an approach to understanding human behavior that divides each person's behavior into child, parent, and adult characteristics. In a nutshell, transactional analysis says that adult behavior is rational and based on one's best interests. Parent and child behaviors are based on emotional thinking. In the late 1970s Coogler developed "structured mediation" and trained hundreds of divorce mediators in his techniques. He was an ardent enthusiast of divorce mediation long before most people ever heard of it.

Coogler viewed mediation as a way to move from the full part-nership of marriage to the more limited partnership of parenthood. He called structured mediation a new form of mediation because it created a self-contained system under which issues are defined and options examined in the light of their probable consequences. If the parties could not settle through mediation, Coogler encouraged them to arbitrate. He appropriated the arbitration rules of the American Arbitration Association, simply substituting Family Mediation Association in the text. This was not done maliciously. Coogler sincerely believed he was contributing to domestic peace and that arbitration avoided the use of impasse as a bargaining strategy.

Many family mediators have been trained in the Coogler tra-dition, especially in the expanded versions described by Sarah Childs Grebe in her article "Building on Structured Mediation" (1994). She calls the modernized version an integrated model of family mediation; arbitration is no longer prominent in it. Arbi-tration has many benefits, but it is best used in family mediation only when the parties have adopted it voluntarily or inserted an arbitration clause in their separation agreement.

The possibility of impasse is an essential part of negotiations. Without it a reluctant party has no reason to compromise. Over-hanging any impasse is the threat that the other party will go to court, and this motivates both parties to negotiate. Various con-cessions may be offered in exchange for a promise not to sue. Medi-ation is a voluntary process; thus the parties should not be required to commit themselves to arbitration in advance.

Arbitration clauses in the final separation agreement are another matter. Such clauses can resolve disputes over designated areas of controversy that the parties anticipate in the future. The courts enforce arbitration clauses, which are used extensively in business; they resolve disputes arising out of the carrier contract. Arbitration is less often used to resolve bargaining impasses to reach the separation agreement.

If the only remaining issue between the parties is who will get Aunt Tilly's tea pot, there may be no reason not to flip a coin, but if the question has to do with the amount of child support and the parties are far apart, MEDALOA is a better choice. The mediator wants the parties to settle their dispute, and there is nothing unethical about suggesting such an alternative. Whether the goal is achieved through settlement or MEDALOA, the clients will have come to a resolution.

Arbitration and MEDALOA involve risks for the clients, and by this point in the discussions a mediator should have a fairly accurate view of the parties' attitudes toward assuming risk. People are less averse to risk than one might expect, particularly when a dispute is boiled down to a question of money. People gamble thousands of dollars on the stock market or the roulette table. Why not on spousal support?

But not every case can be settled. No matter what the mediator suggests, some people will refuse to settle. A mediator who decides that settlement is not possible may have to terminate the mediation by resigning. The parties are then free to negotiate on their own or to find another mediator. Or, if all else fails, they can go to court.

Sometimes a mediator may be reluctant to let go, feeling responsible for the parties' future. A few words of caution from an experienced mediator: "For some, the temptation to attempt to play God proves overwhelming. The parties should be made responsible for their own actions. It is not up to the mediator to tell them how to run their lives. At most, the obligation is to provide them with an informed choice."

Some small percentage of cases have to be resolved in court, usually when one or both parties are unusually stubborn or when the mediator discovers something that makes settlement impossible or inappropriate. Physical abuse of a spouse or child, or substance abuse by a party, may call for court protection or other legal action, not mediation. When a mediator sees evidence of any of these, the parties should be told to seek legal advice so that their rights can be protected. An experienced mediator should be able to identify these sorts of cases.

Step Eight: Finalizing the Agreement

The mediator has a limited role in implementing the final agreement. When the parties have settled their dispute, the mediator should memorialize their agreement in writing, noting the areas of initial agreement and those resolved through mediated negotiations. This is called the memorandum of agreement.

A problem may arise when a final agreement has been memorialized but not yet converted into a signed contract: one party may have second thoughts. In such a case further haggling is not unusual, but the mediator can try to convince the parties they should comply with their original terms of agreement. If the dispute concerns specific language or the legality of a particular clause in the contract, further negotiating can take place with the attorneys.

The formalizing of the separation agreement can also be left to the parties' attorneys, but sometimes disputes will arise when converting the memorandum into a legal document or when new issues are injected by an attorney. Until the parties have signed a formal document, there is always a possibility of further controversy. The mediator should continue to be available to meet with the clients until the formal separation agreement is signed.

An attorney asked to review a mediated agreement may approach it as if it were any other contract that has been negotiated but not yet executed, or may see it as an opportunity to negotiate further. This raises interesting questions. Is the lawyer's responsibility limited to reviewing the legality of the contract? Should a lawyer attempt to determine whether a better deal could have been negotiated? Or even whether the mediator did a competent job?

Sometimes a lawyer wants to renegotiate even if the client is content. The lawyer may question whether the client understood the agreement's legal implications or may criticize certain aspects of it. The client may say that the mediator gave a different impression. Should the lawyer complain to the mediator or try to negotiate with the other party's attorney? The possibility for further dispute is obvious.

The mediator may have to explain the agreement to one of the attorneys, perhaps attempting to justify some of its provisions. In doing so, it may be learned that the lawyer believes the mediator has been negligent. To avoid this kind of thing, some mediators, with the approval of their clients, make it a practice to keep the attorneys informed during the course of the mediation, sending them periodic letters describing the progress of the negotiations.

If the mediator's memorandum is unclear, a reviewing attorney may have legitimate concerns. At the very least, the lawyer must clarify the language, perhaps asking the mediator to explain the agreement. The mediator may have to meet with both attorneys to clear up any ambiguities or technical problems that have arisen. Once again, all this must be done with the clients' approval.

Some attorneys are uncomfortable when clients negotiate agreements without legal counsel involved. Lawyers like to control their clients, but in mediation the parties negotiate for themselves. There is always a possibility of conflict. In a few states where the courts sponsor family mediation, such as Florida, Georgia, Texas, and Maine, it has been customary for lawyers to attend mediation sessions. When asked why that is necessary, Florida attorneys gave various reasons in a survey: to see that the mediator is impartial, to cooperate with the process, to learn how mediation works, and other rationales. The same survey showed that 94 percent of the lawyers think mediation encourages settlement, 79 percent think it saves money, 64 percent think it saves time, and 63 percent think it protects the interests of children (Harrell, 1995). These generally positive views may indicate that attending mediation hearings has educated Florida lawyers about the benefits of family mediation. Still, most family mediators would prefer to deal directly with the parties rather than have attorneys intervene.

Step Nine: Executing the Formal Document

It may be prudent to have the formal separation agreement and other documents sent to the mediator's office by the attorneys to ensure that they conform to the settlement. The formal signing then can take place in the mediator's office. A practical advantage of this to the mediator is that execution of the agreement can coincide with the final payment of the mediation fees.

The formal separation agreement has to be submitted to the family court for approval as part of a divorce petition. That document must conform to statutory requirements before the divorce will be approved. The parties' understanding of their agreement should be reflected in whatever formal documents are prepared.

Some mediated agreements, however, don't need to be incorporated in a formal legal document. For example, a settlement between parents and a teenager about allowance, use of the family car, or curfew can be written down and posted on the kitchen wall. This is a seemingly trivial agreement, but one that may resolve dozens of emotional squabbles during the school year. If the agreement does not have to be reviewed by attorneys or enforced by a court, there may be no necessity for a formal document. The agreement memorandum prepared for the clients is probably sufficient.

Life After the Agreement

Execution of the formal separation agreement terminates the mediator's responsibilities, but sometimes the parties may want to come back when they encounter another disagreement. The Academy of Family Mediators warns that maintaining other professional relationships with the clients after the mediation is concluded may compromise the mediator's neutrality. It is not appropriate for a mediator to serve one of the parties as an attorney or therapist later, even if otherwise qualified to do so. This does not apply, however, to subsequent service as the same parties' mediator or arbitrator.

The mediator may be named in the separation agreement as arbitrator for later disputes if they arise between the parties; as mentioned earlier, arbitration clauses in separation agreements are fairly common. Such clauses often refer to the rules of an administrative agency such as the American Arbitration Association or may name a trusted friend of the parties as the designated arbitrator. If the clients ask their mediator to act as their arbitrator later, that is permissible, but the mediator should not pressure clients to create such a continuing relationship.

Some mediators try to help their clients cope with future problems in their relationships. For some parties this may be valuable, but mediators should recognize that mediation is normally used for help with a current controversy, not for continuing therapy. A mediator should not assume the role of family therapist. Whatever relationships are established during the mediation should terminate after the agreement is signed. Former mediation clients should not become law clients, patients, or even social friends.

After the divorce petition has been filed, it is natural for a mediator to wonder how the divorce or separation worked out. But it is best not worry about that. According to the Academy of Family Mediators, mediation need only result in a "consensual and informed settlement." Fairness is not guaranteed, and for practical reasons: one of the parties may later attack the settlement in court. This occurs infrequently, but there is always a chance that a judge will overrule what the parties have agreed to. Setting potential liability aside, a mediator should not have to demonstrate the fundamental fairness of an agreement that was actually negotiated by the parties, not by the mediator.

On the other hand, the mediator's professional reputation will be based on how clients evaluate their settlements. If a client feels something should have been done differently, it may be bad for the practice. On the practical question of restraining clients from stampeding into a genuinely unwise agreement, the Academy of Family Mediators recommends encouraging them to talk to their lawyers. Perhaps the most prudent policy of all is to

always take them through the nine steps outlined above. Mediators who do so can virtually never be accused of rushing clients
into a settlement.

Sometimes a client will renege on the entire agreement, even
after the divorce; a former spouse who agreed to provide generous
child support may stop working and move to Mexico with a new
sweetheart. In family disputes as in business, there is no guarantee
that people will comply with the agreements they make. With no
advance indications during bargaining, a mediator can't accurately
anticipate whether people will live up to their commitments.
Clients can act in surprising ways; it may seem strange that a person might not know whether to trust a former spouse, but it is very
difficult to forecast that someone will fall in love, remarry, take on
additional family responsibilities, and decide to renege on prior
commitments. In coming to settlements, perhaps the motto should
be that a bird in the hand is better than a migratory ex-spouse.
Many fathers fail to honor their child support commitments.

Calling in the Lawyers

When legal issues arise in negotiations, the mediator should
encourage clients to seek independent legal advice. If they need
extra time to discuss the issue with their attorneys, they should take
it; the negotiations can move forward on other issues. Mediators
must avoid the mistake of telling clients that there is no need to
consult with a lawyer, which is like waving a red flag in front of a
bull in a pinstripe suit. The relationship between attorney and
client is extremely sensitive.

The Academy of Family Mediators makes the point over and
over again, and for obvious reasons. The future of family mediation
may depend upon whether bar associations allow mediators to
manage and control their clients' negotiations. Family mediators
don't practice law, they offer an alternative service; and if bar associations are not enthusiastically supportive, so far they at least
acquiesce. The quid pro quo is that mediators allow lawyers to

advise their clients, formalize final separation agreements, and handle divorce petitions. Thus the academy's adamance on the topic.

Face-to-face negotiations are unquestionably stressful. Sometimes parties need time to cool off or reconsider their positions, so the mediator should never give the impression of rushing them into settlement. Encouraging clients to talk to their attorneys is a way to demonstrate that slower progress is acceptable.

The Academy of Family Mediators encourages mediators to respect complementary relationships with other professions and to promote such cooperation, a wise policy for a relatively new professional association that is trying to develop a service niche. When O. J. Coogler created structured mediation he recommended that parties retain an advisory attorney to draft the final document, file the divorce petition, and complete the formalities. He compared that to what an attorney does when a commercial partnership is being dissolved: represent not the partners, only the partnership. Such an advisory attorney approach might be valid in some states but challenged in others. The Academy of Family Mediators encourages the use of independent legal advice in formalizing an agreement; the Coogler approach does not meet that criterion.

A somewhat similar approach has been adopted by some team mediators, with the lawyer member of the team providing certain legal services. Not every bar association is likely to approve such a system, so mediators developing their practices should investigate the local bar association rules.

Most family mediators find it useful to stay in close touch with the parties' attorneys to keep them informed about the negotiations. The Academy of Family Mediators encourages this; it is prudent anyway because references may come from those same lawyers. In some communities lawyers are important sources of clients for mediators. Joyce Hauser's *Good Divorces, Bad Divorces* (1995) describes how these and other referrals work; see Chapter Five for more details.

Clients should also be encouraged to keep their attorneys informed. If mediation succeeds, these lawyers will have to review the legality of the agreement anyway as part of the divorce petition; both mediator and clients can make this easier through periodic updates. Specialized information from other professional sources may also be required, such as opinions on tax regulations, insurance, and the value of marital assets. Clients should be encouraged to obtain advice on such subjects if it will help them base their negotiations on comprehensive and accurate information.

Confidentiality is another legal concern of mediators. Most mediators take notes during their discussions with the parties. Some tape a memorandum after each session to help them recall what was discussed. Some even tape the discussions, explaining to their clients that the recording is for the mediator's confidential use and will not be used for any other purpose. But however helpful to the mediator, recording inhibits some people from speaking frankly. It lends formality to sessions when a more informal and candid discussion could provide clues about how the dispute can be resolved. A few mediators go so far as to videotape interviews; even with the clients' approval this is likely to inhibit their willingness to express themselves.

The mediator and the clients have a confidential relationship between them that has been confirmed in court by decisions that indicate a mediator cannot be required to testify about the mediation. Some states have created such immunity by statute. The recommended retainer agreement in this chapter specifically provides that the parties will not name the mediator as a party or witness in any subsequent court proceeding, nor subpoena the mediator or any of the mediator's records.

Mediators who are requested to testify in court about any mediation should refuse. If subpoenaed, they should contact the Academy of Family Mediators for advice. The academy also offers professional liability insurance to its members that covers negligent acts and errors or omissions in rendering services as a neutral party involved in family disputes. Various levels of coverage are offered, with defense provided even for alleged dishonest, fraudulent, criminal, or intentionally wrongful acts or omissions.

Summary

This chapter answers basic questions about the process of family mediation. After the participants are made to understand how mediation works and have signed a retainer agreement, most mediations should follow a nine-step procedure of making interim arrangements, getting clients to talk, identifying areas of agreement, clarifying pending issues, obtaining information, negotiating, reaching and concluding a settlement, finalizing the agreement, and executing a final document. The mediator must intervene when necessary, but decisions should be made by the clients. Negotiation between the parties in mediation involves both bargaining and collaboration; to further these processes, mediators use several strategies, including, when necessary, the gap-busting technique called MEDALOA. At certain points, negotiation and settlement may also be assisted by the expertise of lawyers and others.

Family mediation can be used to resolve many different kinds of issues, not just divorce. The next chapter, however, deals exclusively with divorce mediation, the most common and best-known area of practice.

Chapter Four

Divorce Mediation

Divorce does not necessarily destroy a family, nor is it always a catastrophe. It may very well be the best alternative for the people involved. But it does involve a substantial change in relationships.

As the percentage of Americans who can afford to marry drops off, divorce may also decline, but so long as individual freedom and romantic expectations dominate the culture, some couples are bound to enter imprudent marriages and subsequently decide to divorce. Setting aside religious considerations, a civil divorce may free the participants to explore new relationships and embrace more fulfilling lives for themselves.

Divorce has become common. According to the *Demographic Yearbook* (United Nations, 1992), half of all American marriages end in divorce (2,371,000 couples married in 1991 and 1,187,000 divorced); about 5 percent (4.73 in 1991) of all existing marriages end each year. It seems inevitable that divorce will continue to be common; even ignoring the self-indulgence of many Americans, there are economic reasons for the recent increase in divorce as well. Most divorces are initiated by women. More women work today than in the past, so they can afford to strike out on their own. For a working woman, marriage may mean that she has to combine her job with taking care of her family, which can be a burden. If the marriage is unhappy, a woman may decide to rid herself of the marital portion of her burden. When marriage is little more than a boring extra job, why not concentrate on the real job, the career for which she gets paid? There are, of course, many other reasons why women seek divorce.

Just as some wives decide to strike out on their own and find out what they have been missing, so do some husbands. The classic case of the executive who abandons his middle-aged homemaker wife to start a new life with a younger woman is only one example. However legitimate the reasons for deciding on divorce, it is certainly true that too many people marry for unrealistic reasons. For those couples, romantic expectations can easily fray around the edges, particularly in large cities where community pressures don't bind them together and where the environment reeks of temptation. Simple incompatibility has become an acceptable rationale for divorce.

Cultural norms have changed, the sexes have become more socially and economically equal, and the rules of the marriage game have been revised generation by generation. Young married couples today often try to raise families while maintaining stressful his-and-hers careers. Marriage can be unexpectedly demanding even at its best.

When a marriage begins to fail, some couples stick together for the sake of their children. Others decide the children will be better off when mom and dad end their bad marriage; indeed, sometimes divorce even makes it possible for parents to improve their relationships with their children. Whether that turns out to be the case, and whether the individuals have happier lives after divorce, often depends upon the terms of separation. Working out a divorce settlement is no small problem, particularly when children are involved. Many issues must be considered, compromises made, and problems resolved. These are the topics of this chapter.

Behind Divorce

A failed marriage involves more than two people. Behind the principals lurk a host of other interests and influences, not only the children of the couple but other relatives, friends, and even business associates who have an interest in the marriage. The husband and wife can cut free of their marriage, but they will maintain ties to their children and many others who were within the marital orbit—most likely including the ex-spouse to one degree or another, perhaps economically or through the children. Thus the problem in designing a divorce: how to let go of the intimate core without destroying the strands that bind an extended family together.

A civil marriage cannot be dissolved without court involvement. The procedure varies from state to state, but usually the couple must obtain a divorce decree from whichever family court has jurisdiction. Before granting a divorce, the court will consider the financial and custodial arrangements of the separation. The decree determines how marital property is to be allocated and how the children will be provided for. The state is interested in all this not only from a humanitarian standpoint, but because it does not want to have to pick up the tab if an ex-spouse or a child is left destitute after a divorce. In effect, the state says, "You can abandon your marriage vows, but only if nobody becomes a burden on society because of it."

That is the theory, but in practice one or both members of a former couple may renege on their obligations, frustrating the precautions of the court. The court's authority to allocate responsibilities is the background against which private negotiations take place between the husband and wife before their divorce is finalized. In some situations, the most difficult issues concern finances; one spouse may want to retain income and property for a new life while the other, usually the parent who will take custody of the children, makes great demands on that income and property. For that matter, they may fight over custody. However the battles over custody and child support work out, the children will be bound by the final agreement.

Of course, sometimes both parents are equally committed to a settlement that will cover the needs of their children; their discussions are amicable and a divorce settlement is easily arranged. Would that this were always the situation! But divorce negotiations tend to be nasty. Divorce ranks high on the list of events that create stress, and the children share in that stress. Children usually know their parents are planning to separate. They may even suspect that they are the cause of it, a misconception that can generate intense guilt and unhappiness.

The Children of Divorce

Children are vulnerable in the divorce arena. Conventional wisdom is that divorce tends to stunt a child's development because the child may feel rejected, but a child may be harmed even more by the bickering that percolates around a bad marriage. Assuming that couples decide to live apart for valid reasons, divorce may result in a happier family, which obviously benefits the children. Whether measured by school performance or social behavior, children raised in nuclear families may not necessarily be better off than those raised by parents living apart. However, authorities continue to argue about the effect of divorce on children, making generalizations on the subject suspect.

In *The Good Divorce* (1994), Constance R. Ahrons argues that divorce is often better for the entire family than continuing an unhappy marriage, that change is inevitable, and that endings are part of life. After extensive research with troubled families, she stresses the importance of minimizing the effect of divorce on children by continuing to maintain positive family relationships within the binuclear family. Ahrons urges mediation for divorcing families rather than family court because it is more likely to create secure kinship relationships for the future. She encourages couples not to think about divorce in negative ways, but to be flexible and willing to compromise.

When divorce takes children by surprise, they may be damaged. But children who understand that their parents are unhappy may welcome it. As Judith S. Wallerstein and Joan B. Kelly describe it in *Surviving the Breakup*:

> When the divorce is undertaken thoughtfully by parents who have
> carefully considered the alternatives; when the parents have recog-

nized the psychological, social and economic consequences for themselves and the children; when they have taken reasonable measures to provide comfort and appropriate understanding to the children; where they have made arrangements to maintain good parent-child relationships with both parents, then those children are not likely to suffer developmental interference or enduring psychological distress as a consequence of the divorce. . . . (But) if the divorce is undertaken primarily as a unilateral decision which humiliates, angers or grieves the other partner; and if the divorce fails to bring relief from marital stress; and if the children are poorly supported or poorly informed or recruited as allies or fought over in the continuing battle; and if the child feels rejected . . . then the most likely outcome for the children is developmental interference and depression [Wallerstein and Kelly, 1980, pp. 316–317].

Just because parents decide their marriage is impossible does not mean their children will agree. Even an unhappy marriage may seem acceptable to the children; it is all they know. Some mediators believe that it is crucial to explain to the children what is happening.

Young children may envision divorce as punishment inflicted by a parent, particularly if the other parent brings them into the hostilities, which is pathetically easy to do. A child may have to blame someone, and if a parent can be blamed the child does not have to take responsibility for the divorce. When one parent hacks away at a child's relationship with the absent parent, it only adds fuel to the fires of blame; even from a selfish standpoint this is unwise when the absent parent will be called upon in a separation agreement to make child support payments.

Too often a child will say something like, "Daddy left me because he didn't love me" which translates into "Daddy left me because I am not lovable. No one can love me." Far better for the parents to explain why their marriage is not working out and that the problem is entirely their fault, not the child's. Some mediators like to talk to the children for this very reason.

Children are seldom asked whether they favor a divorce, usually just which parent they want to live with. Children should not be made pawns in the battle between the parents, a message that divorce mediators should deliver to both parents. In mediation, the emphasis should be on identifying the best interests of the children, not in involving them in the legal controversy.

Mediation or Court?

Divorce lawyers are expected to get everything possible for their clients, to be zealous advocates if not avengers. Their reputations are built on and measured in victories. Adversarial divorce lawyers can become wealthy and are rarely shy about publicity. As tough negotiators, they manipulate the court system to their advantage and become friendly with family court judges. As they are paid to win, who can blame them?

Family court judges are exposed to such battles on a daily basis and sometimes comment on the fact that divorce lawyers are not always gentle persons who serve their clients in an amicable and fair-minded fashion (Hoffman, 1996).

Those kinds of comments may reflect the problem that matrimonial lawyers must fight for their clients and, because children usually do not have their own lawyers, for the clients' children. But as two clients and two lawyers present two conflicting sets of claims, the judge normally becomes the de facto protector of the children's interests. Still, though family court judges have discretion, they get most of their information from the attorneys and thus are not always adequately informed about the needs of the children. Even when they are well briefed, most judges are appointed politically, not because they have special knowledge of family problems; they certainly are not family therapists.

Lawyers may inflame the already fragile relationship between clients by encouraging them to go to war to win the children and other spoils of divorce. To be fair, this attitude may reflect the wishes of their clients, who may tell them to do everything possible to win. No wonder divorce lawyers have a bad name.

Imagine a typical couple with a child or two, married for a dozen years and living together in the suburbs. They are decent people who are not really angry at each other but have fallen out of love and want a divorce. They visit their attorneys. What happens next? Here is one scenario:

The wife's lawyer tells her to protect herself by draining money out of the joint bank account. The husband's attorney advises him to protect himself by canceling his wife's credit cards. Both are warned to leave the negotiating to the lawyers, and told not to talk with their spouses beyond what is necessary to run the household. A few days later the husband goes to the bank for some cash; no money. He is furious. At about the same time, the wife sets out to buy clothes for the children; no credit. She is humiliated.

The lawyers have, in effect, urged their clients to splash gasoline on a smoldering fire. Technically this is not arson, but the devastation may be as great. Still, lawyers have to represent the interests of their clients; they are only doing their jobs. But the highly adversarial system in use today causes almost everyone to become victims of the process. When legal papers start flying and depositions begin, it gets worse. During a contested divorce, some people learn to hate each other.

But what about no-fault divorce, as discussed in Chapter Two? Even with that, the atmosphere in court is often saturated with the desire of one party to punish the other. Fault no longer needs to be proven for divorce to be granted, but the parties still think in terms of fault. Thus lawsuits over equitable distribution, and custody contests when they have to be decided by a judge, still generate hostility between the parties and can drag on for many months. This is particularly common when wealthy clients are involved, as there is an apparent relationship between the depth of the clients' pockets and the length and vigor of divorce litigation.

Some lawyers are not happy about the contentious atmosphere of divorce litigation but feel they have no alternative. Others encourage their clients to mediate, believing it can drain bitterness out of the negotiations. Not that mediated negotiations are not confrontational. They are, but at least the participants deal directly with each other. Mediation encourages a collaborative relationship on issues that do not need to be bargained over, and the parties can express their emotions and try to make one another understand their needs and expectations.

Until recently lawyers could represent only one side in a divorce, but now it is possible for a lawyer to act as a mediator and help both sides work things out. Some attorneys are comfortable with that role and have made family mediation part of their practices. Others refer clients to private mediators. A few continue to resist mediation. Overall, the use of divorce mediation is rapidly growing, as is demonstrated by the increase in membership of the Academy of Family Mediators. Tens of thousands of divorce negotiations are being handled this way every year.

Even where the participants have maintained a civilized relationship, the complexity of untangling a marriage can make negotiations difficult; mediation can help. A California case illustrates this. A couple had been trying to untangle their marriage for more than a year before the wife's attorney suggested mediation after becoming concerned about what might happen to her client in court.

The couple had been married for seven years and had a four-year-old son. The husband was a senior manager in a major corporation; the wife worked part-time at a good salary. They were wealthy, owning their home, some securities, rental property, and two cars. Nearly a year before entering mediation, the wife had filed for divorce and the court had ordered the couple to continue living together, which was becoming inconvenient. For mediators, the couple retained a psychologist and a lawyer, both of whom were present for all the mediating sessions. The psychologist made sure the clients understood each other and helped them with emotional issues; the attorney explained legal aspects of their negotiations and also explained the tax consequences of proposed settlement terms.

At the first mediation session, the parties were asked to sign a retainer agreement, acknowledging that the attorney did not represent them except as a mediator (when a mediation team includes a lawyer, this may guard against later assertions of a conflict of interest). The most difficult problem was custody. After extended discussions during which the parties strenuously argued over where the child would live, they agreed on joint custody, the son staying with his mother for three days each week including the weekend and with his father the rest of the time. The couple agreed to share child support. Spousal support for the woman would diminish over several years as she became self-sufficient. After eight sessions over six months, all the issues between the clients were resolved. Several sessions had been devoted to untangling the couple's interests in various investments, but the allocation of marital assets was finally decided upon and the final agreement was sent to the clients' attorneys for review and approval.

Mediation often improves relationships between even previously hostile married partners as they prepare to divorce. The court process, on the other hand, almost always inflames relationships by feeding on the hostility generated by most deteriorating marriages.

According to John Haynes, "Mediation won't work for couples who are out to kill each other, but it's ideal for those who prefer a nonadversarial process. I see mediation becoming the first choice for one third of the couples seeking to settle a divorce dispute" (Haynes, 1984, p. 218). Haynes may have been too pessimistic. Most couples are willing to compromise and if given a chance prefer to solve their own problems. Many can do so amicably even without help; divorce mediation is for those who are able to talk about their problems but need professional help in finding solutions.

When couples are so angry that they can only communicate through lawyers, mediation may be out of the question. For people whose primary goal is to punish their spouses, litigation may be exactly what they want. As one divorce lawyer puts it, "I am not worried about mediation taking away my practice. In my community, there are plenty of people who like to fight. When they get fed up with their marriage, I can give them a new outlet for their aggression."

That attorney handles a few cases at a time, a modest percentage of the thousands of couples who divorce in his area. Family mediation is for most of the rest: people who want to minimize the negative impact of divorce on themselves and their children.

Domestic relations cases are a majority of the civil cases in state courts, and divorce litigation is a large part of that. Fortunately, more and more separations are being arranged through mediation; after the parties have come to an agreement, the court need only approve what the parties have agreed upon with the help of a mediator. Family courts are relieved of having to try noncontested divorces, to the benefit of virtually everyone.

The Process of Divorce Mediation

The purpose of divorce mediation is to facilitate settlement, not to encourage divorce or, for that matter, reconciliation. In a few cases, however, mediators may help bring about reconciliation. A trial separation may convince the parties that they should reunite, in which case the mediator can attempt to help them deal with the issues that seem to have driven them apart. By identifying chronic problems and helping the couple to communicate, a mediator may indeed help save a marriage.

Generally, though, mediation is a way to amicably reach a foregone conclusion. Some divorce negotiations are particularly stressful because the parties have not yet accepted their emotional separation even though they have agreed to divorce. One or both may not yet have learned the etiquette of separation, which involves the suspension of intimacy. Becoming separated is the reverse of courtship; instead of pressing forward, the parties must learn to stay appropriately distant from each other.

When clients first come to mediation, the mediator must be frank about that, perhaps telling them something like this: "I'll be asking you both to do something difficult, which is to get it into your heads that you're no longer tied to each other. You'll be living apart and making your own decisions. It may be hard and it might make you angry and unhappy, but you will have to make that transition during these negotiations."

Couples should not expect a miracle. A mediator can guide them through a process that is likely to result in a settlement, but each party must be willing to make concessions. Mediation does not make people like each other. Whatever problems they had before the mediation are likely to be there when it is over. What they learned about each other during years of marriage is not going to change during the relatively few hours they spend with a mediator. Mediators are not magicians; they can help with the process, but the parties must eventually agree between themselves.

One mediator describes her services this way: "My clients are usually sick of fighting. As a mediator, I will do my best to help them collaborate with each other in creating a constructive plan for their future. That is all I can do. The heavy lifting, they have to do for themselves." That is the crux of divorce mediation.

A common problem is that the parties have become so emotionally intertwined during their marriage that they can't let go. They have to cut one strand after another until they become free individuals. People marry because they share certain expectations. When those expectations change, as they almost inevitably do, the individuals may no longer be compatible; at some point they realize their marriage is dead and want to move on. A mediator can help them sever their legal and emotional relationship with the least amount of anguish.

If one of them cannot talk about the future or participate in making plans, it may be an indication that emotional separation has yet to occur. The mediator may have to help such a party become independent, which is a tall order: the person has memories of better times and grieves over the dead marriage. But the mediator should only empathize and show understanding, never sympathize. Grief at such times marks the passage to another way of life as the person discards the intimacy of the unhappy marriage and moves on to an unknown but perhaps happier future.

Clients may have expectations of life after divorce that are far from realistic. They may anticipate a lifestyle of excitement and rejuvenation, or of free time and romance. For most divorced couples it won't happen. Money will be scarce. Those with children will still have parental duties. When the couple meets after divorce they may still argue, and when they are apart they may still be lonely. The mediator should warn clients to be realistic about their postdivorce expectations.

When the parties are ready to confront their future realistically, a mediator can help them by following the general sequence of events described in Chapter Three. Some matters, however, are specific to divorce mediation, and how divorce mediators practice depends upon their perception of the kind of service that best meets the needs of their clients. Some devote primary attention to the arrangements that clients make for their children after divorce. Others include training and counseling of clients as part of the mediation regimen, a process that resembles family counseling.

In one typical case where the mediator used family counseling techniques, a couple with two children was referred to mediation by their attorneys after custody negotiations broke down. They were already living apart. The husband wanted legal custody and equal time with the children, but the wife refused to allow the children to stay with him overnight because he was living with another woman.

At the first joint session the mediator, a family therapist, concluded that the husband and wife were at different stages of emotional development and recommended that both attend a group program for parenting that she offered at her training center. She felt that they would come to understand each other by working together in such a group. As the couple also had unequal bargaining skills, she also suggested that mediation sessions be interspersed with independent study, including the reading of articles about parenting. During the following weeks, the mediator made a home visit to each client to discuss their bargaining positions. At the wife's house, she was able to talk to the children about their preferences and expectations.

At the mediator's suggestion, interim living arrangements were made for a trial period, during which the clients maintained a record of how the plan worked in practice. During that period, they also met several times with the mediator to discuss the terms and conditions of a final agreement. After a total of seven sessions, four joint and three separate, the couple agreed that the children would spend 70 percent of their time with their mother and the rest with their father. The husband also agreed to pay family support based on his income and the children's needs. As this extensive mediation went on, the couple learned to collaborate in defining their parental responsibilities.

Other divorce mediators stress monetary issues. For example, one couple with a four-year-old child decided to separate after eleven years of marriage. Financially they were not in good shape: they had been living beyond their means, buying on credit, their fixed expenses exceeded their income, and they had almost no cash reserves. The husband was ready to concede sole custody, but the wife wanted more support than he could afford to pay.

At the end of the first session, the mediator asked each of them to prepare separate budgets to review at the next meeting. Neither budget was realistic, so the discussion focused on their financial problems. With the mediator's help it became clear to both that they would have to sell their home and move into apartments. They were able to work out a formula for sharing what remained after paying off their creditors. Both had to make concessions, but the solution turned on their being able to face economic reality. Through mediation, they were able to understand the narrow range of viable choices and the need for fiscal responsibility. By the end of just two sessions, they reached agreement on custody, visitation, and family support.

Some mediators believe in a rigid order of dealing with mediated issues. For example, with Sarah Grebe's version of structured mediation (Grebe, 1994), which she calls "integrated mediation," the order in which subjects are taken up is tightly controlled. She believes that before deciding which parent will have legal custody, it is best to deal with parenting issues: the daily schedule of the child, what will happen on weekends and vacations, and how to provide for the child's health, education, and religious upbringing. Many parents think a decision on custody will take care of everything else when the opposite may be true, so it may be more sensible to approach parenting issues one by one. Under the Grebe formula, parenting is intentionally the first general subject to be considered because it encourages the parties to adopt a collaborative approach. If they can collaborate about parenting, they are more likely to do so when dividing property and negotiating levels of support.

The Family Home

Most separation agreements must deal with one large asset: the home where the couple has been living. They must decide who will continue to live there, or whether it must be sold so the proceeds can be allocated between them. Because of the value of the property and because they may have lavished attention on it and improved it in various ways, this matter can cause considerable contentiousness. Neither may want to lose the home, but one or both must.

Sometimes a couple continue to share the home during negotiations, which can lead to continuing disputes. The mediator may have to work out an interim protocol under which one of the parties will vacate, pending a final agreement.

Even after one has moved out, title to the property may cause a problem. One spouse may legally own the house or be the named party in its lease or mortgage. A mediator must be able to help clients untangle title documents that were created in happier times. Negotiations not only must determine occupancy but place title in the appropriate name; legal advice may help.

A common problem is a spouse who continues to occupy the home but cannot cover the operating expenses without support payments from the other spouse. The parties will have to prepare a realistic budget for those expenses. What is the condition of the house? Does it need a new roof? The mediator might suggest that the house be inspected to answer these questions. What are the taxes, mortgage payments, heating bills, and other expenses? All should be researched and considered.

A frequent outcome of negotiations is to sell the home and split the proceeds. But if one party is living in it and prefers not to move into another and perhaps less comfortable residence, it is easy to subvert a sale by postponing appointments to show the property or failing to maintain it in a way that attracts purchasers. Even after an agreement has been reached, one party may refuse to sign off on a sale, either to punish the other party or to obtain some final concession. The mediator should suggest that the agreement be designed to be self-executing. By the time the separation agreement is signed, all necessary documents to carry out the terms of the sale should have been executed, so that neither party can frustrate the intention of the agreement. In addition to real estate, this should apply to the transfer of bank accounts, securities, pension rights, and other transactions that are part of the separation agreement. It may be prudent for the mediator to discuss these problems with the parties' attorneys well in advance of closing on the separation agreement.

Child Custody

As observed in Chapter Two, attitudes toward child custody have changed. Children are no longer regarded as belonging to the father; also abandoned is the notion that young children should always be awarded to the mother if she is capable of caring for them. Courts now are more willing to rely on joint custody, some forms of which are described in state laws or court decisions.

In private mediation, parents can be creative about custody, knowing that judges will usually accept whatever arrangements they work out. All else being equal, parents should share responsibility for their children, but far too often custody becomes a contest and a child becomes a prize to be fought over. The couple may argue about who is the best parent, which often comes down to a power struggle.

Some mediators start discussions on this issue by asking parents what plans they have for their children. Have they decided where the child will live? Are they able to share parental responsibility with the other party? What are their ideas about child support? If it becomes clear they have not discussed such questions or are not in agreement, the mediator should encourage them to collaborate, so as not to decide such important matters on the basis of a mere power struggle. They should think in terms of creating a parenting partnership so that the child can continue to enjoy a healthy relationship with both parents. That is the ideal, but unfortunately many couples prefer to bargain rather than collaborate over custody issues. Still, bargaining is probably better than going to court.

When couples separate, their total living expenses are likely to increase. The expenses of the parent with custody may continue much as before, but the absent parent also needs to live. Many ex-spouses find it difficult to make support payments while also paying for their own living expenses, so some divorced couples spend years bickering over child support.

Child support payments may prove inadequate, a chronic problem among low-income families. One out of every four children in the United States lives with a single parent, usually the mother ("The Family," 1995, p. 6); many of those mothers are poor, supplementing child support with public assistance. Their problems are reflected in state laws that attempt to enforce child support orders through such remedies as payroll deductions and canceling the driver's licenses of those who are delinquent. Mediators need to know what their states' laws provide.

In her book *Mom's House, Dad's House*, Isolina Ricci (1980) encourages a continuing relationship between a child and both parents. She prefers joint custody to avoid situations where one parent wins custody but has to take full responsibility for bringing up the children, while the other loses but must continue to pay even though the children have been taken away. Ricci believes that sole custody generates acrimony between the parents. By denying access to a child, one parent may reduce the other's willingness to pay for their support. In any case, the relationship between the absent parent and the child may stretch and snap.

Joint custody has many adherents. There are endless variations on the theme: the child stays in one house during school days, the other on weekends and vacations; one month in one home, the next in the other; alternating years; the child stays in one home, but the parents switch; or an open schedule, subject to negotiations.

In her book, Ricci makes the following points:

- The parents are divorcing each other, not their children.
- Each parent should continue parental responsibility.
- A parent should not interfere in the other's approach to child rearing.
- Each parent should maintain an appropriate home for the children.

Joint custody is not for every family. Not every couple can provide two living quarters for their children. For some, it may be a struggle to provide even one. Others may be unwilling to accept the continuing responsibility. Joint custody may embroil them in a constant battle over their rights, fighting over and over again, sometimes to the point that one parent, often the father, abdicates parental responsibility and gives in.

Ricci's book, however, contains sound advice for well-intentioned parents, showing how they can be uncoupled from intimacy while continuing to provide joint parenting. She encourages a responsible postdivorce relationship, something that mediation is intended to nurture.

Parents may think that fighting for custody will demonstrate their love for their children, but they are wrong. Their goal should be to work out a sensible arrangement for meeting their children's needs. This can be one of the major benefits of family mediation: helping the parties carry out their parental responsibilities.

Anne L. Milne has written extensively on settling custody disputes. Her technique of "family self-determination" uses a neutral person she calls a counselor, but the process is essentially the same as mediation. The parents agree in advance to participate, discuss their mutual problems in sessions, and attempt to recapture the positive aspects of their relationship (Milne, 1978). Each parent suggests an optimum plan for the child's life. What is best for the child? What is best for the parents? The counselor talks to the children, trying to discern what would be good for them and what they prefer. Then the counselor tries to help the parties reach agreement. Later the counselor provides follow-up counseling.

Milne is convinced that family self-determination provides a better solution to custody than can be achieved in court, where a judge may rely almost exclusively on a mental health professional's recommendation. Moreover, parents who go to court for a decision are often back in court within two years; Milne says her system costs less and puts less stress on the family than using a more adversarial process.

Not everyone is willing to deal with custody issues amicably. Some want to punish their spouses and are willing to sacrifice their children in the attempt. Family mediation is not for them.

Sometimes mediation over custody fails at first and succeeds later. For example, one couple with three teenagers had been married for twenty-two years but recently separated. The husband had filed for divorce. The wife did not want a divorce, but had been having trouble controlling the children, particularly the oldest son. A court psychologist recommended that the boy live with his father; the judge agreed, but allowed the two younger girls to stay with their mother pending an evaluation, which subsequently recommended shared custody, with the children to live with the father. The judge disagreed, not wanting to separate the children from their mother. At that point, the couple decided to go to a private mediator.

The mother was willing to have her son continue living with his father but wanted the girls to stay with her. The father wanted all of the children to be with him. The mediator discovered that the mother felt rejected by both her husband and her children. The problem with trying to negotiate in mediation was that she hoped for a reconciliation. By refusing to compromise, she thought she could block the divorce; she was using mediation as a way of maintaining her relationship with her husband, and had no intention of reaching any agreement because doing so would confirm their separation. Whenever she seemed on the verge of making a concession, she would talk with her parents or her attorney and come back with a rejection. Mediation failed.

The parties returned to court. Another custody evaluation was ordered, which again recommended that the father be given custody of the children. At that point, the mother indicated a willingness to make a deal. They returned to the mediator and were able to agree on a form of joint custody under which the girls would remain with her and the son with the father.

In another apparently failed mediation, the parties still gained insights to settle their differences out of court, if not at the mediation table. The attorneys representing a husband and wife in a contested divorce action had anticipated that their clients would settle quickly. But the case dragged on, tentative agreements kept falling through, and the lawyers knew it would be an unpleasant trial if court was involved. They recommended mediation.

The couple, who had children, had been married for twenty years and separated for about a year. As a sales manager, the husband made almost three times as much money as his wife, a secretary. Their property included a house with a large mortgage on it, a few investments, life insurance, two used cars, and personal property.

The mediator quickly saw that the initial problem was to restrain their bickering. Even after they were cautioned, they continued to argue. In caucuses, however, the mediator could get them to concentrate on the issues. But even after that, arguments sometimes flared up to the point that the mediator would have to interrupt them and warn them to stop wasting time.

The wife wanted the children to live with her, with visitation rights for the husband. The husband couldn't decide if he wanted custody, but seemed willing to concede on that issue if the house could be sold and support payments were reasonable. She demanded $1,200 in child support and another $400 for herself each month, plus 40 percent of any salary increases her husband might get in the future. He offered a total of $1,000 a month. She then made additional demands: loss of his visitation rights if he ever lived with another woman, and an agreement that he would never open his own business or move out of state. The husband flatly rejected these proposals, the wife began screaming at her husband again, and the mediator adjourned the session.

Before the next session, the mediator received a call from the husband's attorney, who said that his client was not willing to subject himself to further abuse. Unless the mediator could control the wife, his client would abandon the mediation. The mediator agreed that if the next session were not productive, he would declare an impasse, then called the wife to talk about her behavior. At the next session, she apologized for her outburst, explaining that she had needed to get some things off her chest. After that, the couple were able to agree on shared custody of the children.

The mediator noted that they seemed able to collaborate on issues that concerned their children, so when the discussion turned to dividing marital property and bogged down over the sale of the house, the mediator switched them to the issue of child support. They were unable to agree on the figures, however, so the mediator adjourned the session, telling them to rethink their positions and believing that settlement was imminent.

During the interim, the mediator met separately with each party to try to convince them to compromise. The husband seemed willing to make further concessions, but the wife did not. Despite waning optimism, the mediator thought it seemed worthwhile to have one final session. But when it began, the wife demanded a copy of the husband's final proposal and he refused to give it to her until she produced her own. She stormed out of the room; the mediator decided not to call her back, concluding that the mediation had failed.

The mediator prepared a memorandum describing the tentative agreements that the parties had reached, hoping their lawyers would be able to persuade them to settle anyway. They did, only a few days before trial. The agreements reached in the mediation, combined with other concessions suggested by the attorneys, shaped the settlement. According to the mediator, the attorneys were pleased because they didn't have to try the case even though the mediation failed to reach final settlement. During mediation, the couple had begun to learn how to negotiate in a collaborative way, and they carried the lesson outside the mediation room.

Considerations for Divorce Mediators

Learning to talk with and understand clients and children is a matter of experience and technique. Dealing with cases of abuse is another thing altogether. Some matters mediators can handle, but others must be placed in the hands of other experts. That is not to say that situations in which there is some minor abuse cannot be mediated.

Interviewing Children

A mediator may want to talk to clients' children privately on occasion to determine their attitude on custody or visitation. This can be done only if both parents agree. Even if they do, the mediator's job is not to make children choose between their parents, but only to see if one plan is more to their liking than another.

If the mediator gains insights from such interviews, how should the parents be told? This can be tricky. In times past, children were regarded as chattel with no say in such matters; even today, some parents don't think that children should be involved in deciding the terms of a separation agreement. Certainly children have no direct voice in the negotiations, and the mediator should not expect children's wishes to determine the outcome.

A child's rejection of a parent may poison the relationship. The mediator must therefore be diplomatic and think carefully how to describe a child interview to the parents. It may be better to preserve the child's neutrality, so that neither parent will enlist the child in the controversy. Children should not have their relationship with a parent jeopardized.

Some children can be invited into the main mediation (once again only with their parents' consent) if they are mature enough. Even then, it may be better for the mediator to talk with the children separately. Some mediators discuss the draft agreement with the children, making certain they understand it. It will affect their lives, but even so not every parent wants the children to be involved. Mediators have various approaches to including the children. Some will talk to them separately. Others allow them to attend some of the sessions, sometimes participating, sometimes not. At times, the parents may be too emotional for the child to be there.

How much weight should be given to a child's opinions? If a four-year-old says she wants to live with her father, does it reflect that mom does the discipline and dad buys the ice cream? Did one parent promise a toy if she gives the mediator the right answers? It is possible, and a mediator should consider such things before relying on what a child says.

Some mediators don't think children should ever be invited into joint sessions. As one put it, "The parents are my clients. They are legally responsible for whatever they decide about their children." On the other hand, the children do have a personal interest. They will have to live under the agreement; after parents separate, the support payments may not be sufficient to provide the children's prior lifestyle. Many divorced parents share such financial concerns with their children. It may be better to do this before the divorce, not after; a child may have to prepare to make sacrifices.

Family mediators who believe in bringing adolescent children into joint sessions think that they should be involved in planning their family's future, exposed to the potential problems, and allowed to participate in finding solutions. As the children have an emotional and economic interest in the results, this seems reasonable enough if the parents approve and it does not interfere with negotiations between the adults.

The Academy of Family Mediators says that family mediators should encourage clients to consider the interests of children and to examine "apart from their own desires" (Academy of Family Mediators Standards of Practice, 1995, VII[B]) their children's separate and individual needs. Accordingly, a mediator should at least raise questions about the children's best interests by bringing the subject to the parents' attention and helping them discuss it. Perhaps clients have overlooked the impact of the agreement on their children, or perhaps they have thought about it and decided to ignore it. Unfortunately, some parents use their children as pawns in the game of divorce.

In court, lawyers sometimes argue over custody or visitation as if they were abstract business deals. In mediation, a more humane approach is appropriate. A mediator should remind the parents that their children have feelings, wishes, rights, and retentive memories. Even young children understand that something is happening when their parents are going through a divorce—something bad. They may feel responsible for it, in which case they must be convinced that they are not to blame so they won't carry emotional scars throughout life. The mediator should try to guard against that by showing clients how their behavior may affect the children. Though they do not directly advocate for the interests of their clients' children, mediators should do what they can to express those interests to the parents in such a way that they are fully considered in the negotiations.

Child and Spouse Abuse

Family mediators sometimes encounter parents who abuse their children. Perhaps the parents too were abused as they were brought up; abusive environments often pass from generation to generation.

In one typical case, the abusive mother was brought up by her mother and aunt. Her mother would come home from work. When she was tired, she would scream at her daughter. The aunt would beat the child. If the girl talked back, the aunt would hit her across the face. The abuse was never reported. That woman abused her own child; she was afraid it would get worse.

That woman was in therapy at a social agency. She claimed a divorce would reduce the stress that was causing her to abuse her child. The agency wasn't so sure, but a volunteer counselor working with the family thought a separation might help because her husband was a violent influence in the home; when he mistreated his wife, she took it out on her child. The agency recommended a divorce.

When child abuse is disclosed, what should a mediator do? Some say that abuse cases should not be mediated, that the mediator should resign. Others believe a mediator might be able to help design a plan that will protect the children, perhaps by giving custody to another person. The woman knew she had a problem; she might have been willing to accept an alternative if one were offered. Abusive people may be willing to give up their children to protect them; it is a mistake to generalize about them. Love can exist alongside abuse, not that the former is any reason to endure the latter.

Temporary stress may cause abuse, such as the loss of a job, substance abuse, health problems, or the pending divorce. Tension within the family may bring about loss of self-esteem and contribute to abuse. Parents under stress may take out their frustration on their children. Eliminating the sources of stress that lead to abuse may be a valid reason for a couple to separate; the mediator may decide that temporary placement of an abused child with another family is proper, pending the final resolution.

Some states require that all cases of child abuse be reported; thus mediators in those areas are obliged to inform the designated authorities if they detect such abuse. In other jurisdictions, the mediator may be able to decide whether the child will benefit from being exposed to the authorities; in some situations, a mediated solution might be better for the entire family.

Much the same comments can be made about spouse abuse as about child abuse. Usually the wife is the victim of spouse abuse; a mediator must make a judgment about its character and extent before deciding if mediation is a possible way to deal with it. Is the abuse physical or mental? Chronic or rare? Brought on by substance abuse or temporary stress? How will the abuse affect negotiations? Will a separation alleviate or eliminate the problem? Are the parties able to negotiate or should the mediator withdraw? Is there a duty to report the situation to the authorities?

The primary consideration, of course, is the abuse victim's safety. Will the mediation add to the risk? If so, the victim's attorney should be advised that mediation is not appropriate. The matter may then be transferred to court.

Using Mental Health Experts

When custody issues arise in court, a judge may request a specialist's professional opinion about the best interests of the child. Usually this involves conducting extensive interviews of the parents, their children, and maybe even friends and neighbors of the family. The expert then attempts to evaluate the parents' suitability for custody. This report may form the basis of the court's decision.

Most parents don't enjoy such investigations and prefer to settle their dispute privately. Rather than requiring an investigation, a mediator talks with the parents about the alternatives so they can determine which would be best for their children. In some situations, a mediator may suggest that a report be obtained from a mental health professional, though only with the consent of the parents. In most circumstances, however, such an examination is unnecessary.

Most parents raise their children without interference from the government. During divorce negotiations they should continue to exercise their right to decide what is best for their children unless they are unable to agree and have to ask a court to decide for them. Whatever changes need to be made in their relationships with their children should be decided by the parents themselves.

Legal Advice on Settlements

The mediator's sole function is to help the clients reach an agreement, but as divorce negotiations usually involve legal issues, a mediator must be familiar with divorce law just as a marine pilot must be aware of the rocks and shoals under a ship channel.

Mediators are quite likely to be asked legal questions by their clients and may be tempted to answer. They can always tell the clients to consult their attorneys, but in the real world mediators do answer certain kinds of legal questions. Some, for example, are willing to express an opinion about how a case might be decided in family court. Others are not.

In general, clients may discuss applicable law with mediators but should then be encouraged to check with their attorneys. Family mediators don't give formal legal opinions because they don't want to be accused of practicing law; they are very careful about that.

In any event, it is difficult to calculate what a court might award for, say, child support. Making such an estimate would require knowledge of the track record of particular family court judges, and it is unlikely that a mediator knows such a thing. The task is thus better left to the party's attorney. In Texas, some divorce mediators confer with the attorneys in advance and compare estimates, but that is not common in most other parts of the country. A mediator should be familiar with child support guidelines but is not generally expected to know what a particular judge is likely to award.

Summary

Divorce mediation has aspects that are not always present in less formal kinds of family mediation. A divorce mediator works with clients who know each other very well from their marital relationship but are likely to be angry at each other, particularly at the outset of the mediation. A mediator has the initial challenge of turning the parties away from their bottled-up hostilities and toward collaboration on a sensible readjustment of their lives.

Family mediators can help couples survive separation. A couple who can negotiate a settlement through mediation are likely to find their divorce less painful than if they litigated the issues in court. The benefits to children are also considerable, as mediation encourages considering their best interests.

A divorce mediator needs to be familiar with the full range of issues that arise when a marriage is being dismantled, from the human complexities of custody and visitation to the complicated financial and legal aspects of property transfer. The mediator must not only understand applicable legal doctrines, but have a deep understanding of the psychological concerns that are found in discordant families. Above all, the mediator must be able to persuade parties to resolve their disputes not just through bargaining, but by means of collaboration.

Learning how to mediate divorces involves knowledge, experience, and a strong personality. In the next chapter, the reader will learn how and consider whether to become a family mediator.

Chapter Five

How to Become a Family Mediator

If you believe at this stage that family mediation is simple and can be practiced by any reasonable person, I have failed to explain its complexity and the subtle skills needed to bring people together in a highly emotional arena.

A mediator must bring experience, adroitness, and sensitivity to the table. Moreover, attempting to help families in this way can be a thankless task. If the parties are successful, they often take full credit for their success and the hard work of the mediator is soon forgotten. Since the entire process is confidential, no one will ever know how brilliantly you brought the parties together. Mediators are prohibited from publicizing their successful cases, so all they have at the end of the day is the pleasure of having helped a few people resolve their disputes.

If the parties make a mess of their negotiations, they are likely to blame the mediator, forgetting they were warned that it is their responsibility to find a solution. It is a no-win situation.

Nor is family mediation a particularly profitable occupation. Most mediators practice part-time, fitting mediation cases into whatever their primary occupation may be. They charge the clients an hourly rate, usually quite a reasonable one, and most of the hours they charge for are spent in direct contact with the clients. As the cases I have described indicate, the amount of time spent by a mediator on a particular case can vary from an hour or two for a single meeting on a simple matter, to lengthy periods for multiple joint and private meetings on complex cases. Mediators must give clients personal attention, so they can't leverage their incomes by having associates do some of the work. Nor can they charge contingency fees or base their fees on how much money is involved in the controversy.

Frequently, the work does not come in on a regular basis. It is difficult for family mediators to achieve a regular working schedule. For the convenience of clients, some sessions may have to be scheduled for evenings or weekends; no matter when they are scheduled, clients often cancel when they encounter other priorities. As negotiations move toward settlement, the pressure on the mediator becomes more intense. Final closure may not take place until late in a session, when the parties are tired and decide to make the last few crucial concessions before they are totally worn out. By then, the mediator may be exhausted.

It is stressful dealing with clients who dislike each other, don't trust each other, or don't like being finessed into an agreement. Guiding participants through negotiations under those circumstances can be unpleasant work. Family mediators sweat. Don't expect your clients to become your friends. They may never want to see you again because you will remind them of a difficult time. If you are a lawyer, they will never become your clients. If you are a therapist, they will never be your patients.

As one mediator explained, "There are no easy cases. My clients are too caught up in their own problems and too embittered for mediation to be anything more than a hassle."

What kind of person would want to enter such a difficult profession, to make such sacrifices for others? Why would you want to spend your time resolving other people's disputes? If you are thinking of joining the field, these questions are worth asking and the answers are worth searching for.

Do You Really Want to Mediate?

You have to decide for yourself. I know many family mediators who say they enjoy what they do. They complain about the difficulties but find satisfaction in helping others. I have tried to understand why. These are my conclusions.

Some family mediators like the control they exert over clients, although control may be too strong a word. At most, a mediator can direct in a tentative way. A mediator can't bully or openly criticize clients or they might walk out of the room. A mediator's only weapon is persuasion.

A mediator can't be opinionated, at least not to clients. For lawyers especially, that can be difficult. Attorneys are taught to make judgments about liability and fault. When they serve as mediators, they have to restrain themselves from being judgmental and accept the clients as they are, not as they ideally might be. Mediators must remain neutral, allowing the parties to negotiate their own settlements. Can you exercise that much restraint?

A famous trial lawyer once told me why he could not serve as a mediator. "Every part of me has been programmed to take sides. Not a great characteristic, I suppose, but when you have looked at issues as a partisan for twenty years, you can't suddenly change."

A family mediator's primary responsibility is to persuade people to commit themselves to a practical and enduring arrangement for their future, what the Academy of Family Mediators calls an "informed and voluntary settlement." The settlement may not be popular with interested third parties, but the mediator has no direct obligation to them other than to see that their needs have been considered by the clients. The mediator works exclusively for the parties at the table, not for third parties or for the public. Other interests should be considered but need not be reflected in the agreement. It would be pointless, of course, for the clients to enter into a solution that third parties will (and have the power to) reject, but the selfish interests of the clients play the dominant role in the design of the settlement agreement. So long as the arrangement is not illegal, the parties have a right to impose upon the interests of others. Does that bother you?

Say, for example, that your clients have a daughter who is president of her class at a famous prep school and an excellent scholar. She is also seeing a psychiatrist. In their negotiations, her parents agree that she will have to give up analysis because they no longer want to pay for it. She is heartbroken, but her parents explain that they have other priorities. In order to maintain their lifestyle, someone has to make a sacrifice. You think they are being selfish. Are you willing to abide by their decision anyway?

What if the parties won't take time to consider all of the complexities of their situation and rush into an imprudent agreement? As their mediator, you warn them that they are making a mistake, but they persist. What should you do?

One mediator put it this way: "Sometimes parties stampede for the barn. I have to stop them because they have not dealt realistically with their problems. It takes time for people to rearrange their lives. I have to be sure that they have done their work."

Are you willing to defer to your clients' judgment? According to the Academy of Family Mediators, "The primary responsibility for the resolution of a dispute rests with the participants" (Academy of Family Mediators Standards of Practice, 1995, VII[A]). But what if you are certain that something terrible will happen? Just because the parties are willing to sign an agreement does not mean that a long-term solution has been achieved. You may anticipate that one of them will default, either because the commitment was not made in good faith or because of future events that you anticipate. The settlement you helped to achieve may become a worthless piece of paper. Will that bother you? Are you willing to let your clients make mistakes?

This sort of introspection should be done before you embark upon a career in family mediation. Consider the kinds of clients who will come to you for help. You must be prepared to allow them to make their own decisions, even if their agreements are selfish or impractical. It is not the mediator's function to make substantive decisions for the parties. Are you willing to submit to their judgment?

Qualifications for Family Mediators

A mediator must care about the clients. That is crucial, but there are other important criteria. A mediator must exhibit integrity and impartiality, be able to gain client confidence, and conduct skillful interviews to dig out information. A mediator must be open-minded and able to work with different kinds of people. Family problems arise in fascinating variety, reflecting all facets of society and those who dwell in it. If you don't like to work with some kinds of people, you may not be suited for the job. Your clients should feel that you respect them and believe them to be important.

Mediators must be able to lead people through the frustrations of the negotiating process. Accordingly, they need patience. Negotiations can get bogged down over seemingly trivial matters, but the parties need time to rummage through relevant information at their own pace. If you get bored easily, you should look elsewhere for a vocation.

Mediators should have a working knowledge of personal finances and family law. Some of that may come from professional training, but experience may be the best teacher. Good mediators acquire necessary information as easily as a sponge takes in water. As technical questions arise, a mediator should be capable of consulting with family counselors, lawyers, accountants, and other experts, which means developing a professional network. Access to a good library with books on the law is essential.

In Chapter One, I mentioned the four primary areas of expertise that a family mediator must bring to the table: dispute resolution, law and finance, family organization, and the ability to work effectively with clients. But a competent family mediator must be familiar with many other subjects that might be of concern to a family, for clients will expect you to know when an issue deserves further attention.

A family mediator works on a very personal level. Words, gestures, facial expressions, and periods of silence provide clues to communication. Pieced together, they form a meaningful pattern. (As you observe your clients, they will also be watching you.) Try to identify what is happening between them. You must be able to intercept the kinds of fleeting messages that are expressed in a shrug, a raised eyebrow, or a frown. When a client begins to cry, you have to know what is being communicated.

It is hard work. A mediator may feel dejected at the end of a session where nothing has been accomplished, wondering what could have been done differently. At other times, when the parties have collaborated on an innovative agreement, the mediator may feel quiet satisfaction.

A mediator must be articulate, strong, and logical, capable of solving problems and possessing a keen sense of timing. It is essential to understand the needs and expectations of clients; otherwise you won't be able to bring them together.

Good mediators have a strong desire to help parties solve their problems not through manipulation but persuasion. The goal is to achieve an informed and consensual settlement; when the clients resolve their problem to their mutual satisfaction, the mediation has been successful.

Anyone can claim to be a family mediator simply by announcing a willingness to accept clients—so far there are no licensing requirements. The trick is to get business. In almost every community, family mediators have set up shop. Some have established reputations and serve private clients or in court-based programs. Others are only wanna-bes. The lawyers and family service agencies know the family mediators in their communities who have a good reputation for their work with clients. You should identify such mediators and organizations in your community; as with any profession, networking is essential.

Where Can You Get Training?

Training seminars for family mediators are now widely available. The Academy of Family Mediators maintains an approved list of other training organizations. Many of them provide forty- or sixty-hour basic training, with additional specialized seminars and workshops available. The academy itself provides conferences for its members where leading family mediators lecture on specific subjects. Local mediation groups offer similar training programs. The Academy of Family Mediators encourages family mediators to acquire such training.

The training programs available to family mediators not only stress needed skills but illustrate the mediation process through mock sessions supplemented by lectures and demonstrations. Training may not by itself turn out fully qualified family mediators, but it certainly provides an opportunity to acquire knowledge of the field.

Some family mediators are calling for more extensive training. Alison Taylor's (1994) article "The Four Foundations of Family Mediation Training: Implications for Training and Certification" illustrates the trend: "Acquisition of the knowledge and skills necessary to become an effective family mediator in helping children and adults with issues that profoundly impact their families depends on more than cursory training" (p. 89).

In calling for more elaborate systems of training and supervised practice, Taylor probably presages a push toward mandatory training and certification. Mediators who serve in family court programs are already subject to various court-mandated requirements; private family mediators can expect similar criteria will be imposed upon them, particularly if state licensing laws are passed. The Academy of Family Mediators already imposes various educational requirements for becoming a "practitioner" of the academy as opposed to a subscribing member. A practitioner must complete sixty hours of mediation training, have one hundred hours of face-to-face mediation experience in at least ten actual cases, submit six sample memoranda or reports about those cases, and complete twenty hours of continuing education every two years. The content of the mediation training is described in some detail by the academy.

The relevance of this to someone who wants to become a family mediator is that entrance to the profession in the future may demand greater commitments of time and money. Before embarking on family mediation as a career, you should investigate the situation in your state and decide what level of commitment you are willing or able to make.

A family mediator is expected to participate in continuing education and professional growth. As a practicing mediator, your problem is to find programs that will fit your particular needs. The

Academy of Family Mediators lists a substantial number of organizations that provide training in family mediation. Some of those programs include internships that give some limited experience.

The available training varies in quality. The Academy of Family Mediators recommends that potential trainees find out how many programs a particular facility has carried out. Are the trainers experienced family mediators? Read what they have published in the field. Is posttraining supervision and follow-up available? Does the training include an internship? How many graduates of the program have become active family mediators? Ask questions like these before signing up.

In addition to training, it is important to gain experience. You might offer to serve as a volunteer with a community mediation program. Cases in such programs are somewhat different from those usually encountered in private practice, but working on them will give you useful experience in applying mediation techniques to interpersonal controversies. Serving as a community mediator can be a gratifying volunteer experience and provides an opportunity to determine whether you have the ability to mediate disputes.

As family mediator Mark Lohman of Washington, D.C., points out, "The educational needs of a mediator are highly complex. Not only must the mediator have a knowledge of family law almost comparable to that of a family lawyer, but must be knowledgeable in family therapy issues, especially the impact of divorce on children. One must know about taxes, as well as present-day and long-term finances, including health and life insurance."

In addition to the subjects mentioned by Lohman, you should be familiar with the local employment market. Most families are supported by wages or salaries. The money that makes it possible to solve family problems, to care for children, or for one party to live separately usually comes from a job. A client may have to find employment or seek a new career, as is often the case with housewives after a divorce. A mediator should be familiar with the local employment market, job training programs, and various sources of government support.

The primary wage earner carries a veto in many divorce negotiations. That person can move away, create a new family, withdraw from the labor market, or frustrate a settlement agreement in a hundred other ways. A mediator should be prepared to calculate the likelihood of such eventualities. What do you know about the wage earner's job? About your clients' personal lives? What social structure binds them to the settlement? If the working environment is stable, the support payments may be more secure. For a mediator to understand that relationship requires some knowledge of the working world.

A mediator also needs a knowledge of the tax laws. An innovative solution to a family dispute may involve figuring out how certain taxable transactions can be handled most effectively. By spotting potential tax opportunities, the mediator will know when to send clients to a tax adviser for advice. Some mediators have a knack for reducing the cost of settlements through innovative tax planning. Tax savings may justify a settlement.

Do You Have to Be a Lawyer?

Some family mediators are indeed lawyers, usually ones who specialize in domestic relations law, perhaps as divorce lawyers, and decide to branch out into mediation. They may continue to practice law in the traditional way but add mediation to the menu for clients. Even a few retired family court judges have become family mediators.

In a few states lawyers at one time were not encouraged to serve as family mediators, but when lawyers realized mediation was becoming popular that changed. Bar associations saw that some of their members could serve as mediators and provide a valuable service. By now, they encourage their members to use mediation in their practices.

But lawyers still must differentiate between mediating and providing joint representation. The general rule is that a lawyer approached by a husband and wife in a matrimonial matter can serve as a mediator or arbitrator, but it would not be proper for such an attorney to represent both parties in court.

The Association of the Bar of the City of New York has issued guidelines on mediation stating that clients should be warned that important legal rights are involved in a divorce and be encouraged to retain independent counsel to advise them about the potential risks. That is a typical bar association attitude, consistent with the stance of the Academy of Family Mediators. Whether or not family mediators are lawyers, they should encourage clients to consult attorneys and have them review the mediated settlement memorandum.

After serving as a mediator between two clients, a lawyer must refuse to represent either one individually, or participate in any way, in any subsequent legal proceedings over matters dealt with in mediation.

Lawyers who serve as family mediators should know their local bar associations' policies on family mediation and determine exactly what they are authorized to do. That will avoid the possibility of being challenged on the basis of having provided joint representation.

Sometimes a couple who have worked out the terms of their divorce settlement may ask a mediator to put the agreement in writing. Some bar associations would allow a lawyer to provide such a service, after making a full disclosure of any prior relationships and warning both parties that they should obtain independent legal advice prior to signing the agreement. But it would not be appropriate for a family mediator, whether or not an attorney, to draft a legal agreement in such a way. Drafting legal agreements is practicing law.

Other bar associations have taken the position that lawyers should not draft such an agreement for both parties because of potential conflicts of interest. There are several reasons cited. Clients negotiating a divorce tend to be emotional. Their emotional distress may be so severe that one or both of them may be incapable of understanding the agreement. Furthermore, a lawyer who represents both parties may fail to obtain all necessary information. Finally, a lawyer should not attempt to represent both sides in a conflict situation.

A lawyer can serve as a family mediator if the lawyer discloses all prior relationships with the parties, but should not render legal services to either or both parties under any circumstances. Nor should the lawyer represent either party in a marital dissolution or in any subsequent legal action.

Returning to the basic question in this section: no, family mediators need not be lawyers. There is certainly no requirement that a family mediator have legal credentials or legal training, though many do. Indeed, the legal issues in any given family mediation are often secondary. If the best interests of the children are primary, a family therapist or social worker might contribute more important insights. The case studies cited in this book describe mediations done by attorneys, other specialists, and mixed teams. Clients should be able to choose whatever kind of mediator or team of mediators they mutually desire.

In the United States, with its plethora of attorneys, there is a danger that family mediation will become "lawyerized." The danger is not that attorneys will enter the profession, but that litigation procedures will migrate into the process, converting it from an informal and confidential discussion between the triad of participants into something more like an administrative hearing or adjudication. In some states traces of that are already apparent. Lawyers attend family mediations, claiming to protect their clients; regulations are imposed upon court-appointed mediators; mandatory standards of practice are adopted; mediators are subject to grievance procedures or civil liability. As family mediation drifts toward licensing and self-regulation, can legal standardization and more involvement by lawyers be far behind? Perhaps that would be a good thing. Opinions differ, but you should be aware of the trend.

Domestic relations law is laid out in state statutes and case reports. Family mediators who are not lawyers can take courses and subscribe to professional publications on the subject. It may also be prudent for them to establish professional relationships with knowledgeable lawyers, who can help them stay informed about legal issues.

As mentioned earlier, mediators who are not lawyers can discuss legal topics with their clients but cannot provide actual legal advice. Otherwise a client may later claim to have relied on legal advice from a mediator that turned out to be erroneous, or a lawyer may claim that a mediator was engaging in the unlawful practice of law.

Lay mediators can reduce that risk by telling clients not to rely on them for legal advice but to consult their own attorneys, much as they would consult accountants, property appraisers, and other specialists when other areas of expertise are relevant to negotiations.

Are You Impartial?

The answer is no. Nobody is completely impartial. We all have prejudices, even if we don't recognize them for what they are. We have entrenched opinions about the opposite sex, different cultures, other generations. We like some people and dislike others. Eliminating every vestige of bias is impossible for all but saints; life is too complex to make do without the efficiencies of habitual ways of thinking.

Despite that, mediators have to be neutral in the two-party negotiations over which they preside. As a mediator, your job is to help your clients settle their dispute. Whether they are good people or bad, whether they are being fair to their children, is not the issue. A mediator need have no more concern about the moral character of clients than a mechanic has about the owner of the car getting a tune-up.

Impartiality for a mediator is freedom from favoritism or bias in word or action. A family mediator is expected to serve both parties, not just one, in reaching a mutually satisfactory agreement. Impartiality applies only to word or action; you are not required to personally feel that both parties are wonderful human beings, just to refrain from playing favorites between them. You can mediate for despicable clients, so long as you treat them impartially.

A mediator must not only be neutral but appear neutral, which is why some mediators practice in teams: one male and one female, one lawyer and one family therapist, or some other combination. The theory is that mediators of different sexes or professions seem (and may even be) more impartial.

Combining a lawyer and psychologist may also provide additional insights and flexibility. For example, at the first meeting with clients the lawyer might explain the procedure, define the issues, and provide technical information and define the parties' legal rights; the psychologist might then discuss the options for child custody and division of family property. There is at least one drawback to this: it costs twice as much.

Why would the psychologist on such a team handle the property discussions? Because many property disputes involve symbolic issues. Objects may be real or symbolic. One person may seem rigid about a particular possession, say an automobile. What does it mean? It may represent a cherished memory or an opportunity to punish the other party. Those symbolic considerations may be more understandable to a therapist than to the average attorney.

Team mediation can avoid some ethical and legal problems by allocating responsibility between the team members, but it may raise different concerns. For example, lawyers are not allowed to practice law in association with nonlawyers; fee splitting or sharing of clients with a nonlawyer is prohibited. If a mediation team were to draft a separation agreement and then the lawyer were to process the divorce petition for the clients, the team members might be in trouble on both counts. The therapist might be accused of practicing law without a license and the lawyer of fee splitting. Once again, a mediator should find out how the local bar association regards such matters.

Can a mediator be sued? Certainly. In the current legal climate, there is always a chance, and when mediators do not maintain an appearance of impartiality, the odds of being sued further increase.

Mediators try to protect themselves by emphasizing that their function is not to give legal advice, but the risk of a malpractice claim is always there. Mediators often work with difficult people who can't get along with others. To avoid being added to such individuals' lists of targets for wrath, prudent mediators will be careful not to establish too close a relationship with one client, which might make the other one suspicious. If both sides believe you have been fair and if they are generally satisfied with their settlement, you are less likely to be sued. Also, to the extent that you reduce their anger with each other during the mediation, they may become less hostile toward you as well.

The mediator must try to maintain the confidence of both parties by creating an evenhanded and peaceful atmosphere. Don't take sides. Don't let your clients draw you into their arguments. Maintain your distance. Here are some practical suggestions:

- Call time-out when a client gets emotional.
- Don't condone a physical threat by either party.
- Keep sessions cool and businesslike.
- Don't serve liquor.
- Never, never become intimate with a client!

In addition to the parties, watch out for their attorneys, who may be eager to find fault with what you have been doing either because they are jealous of your relationship with their client or in response to a client's complaint. To guard against this, most mediators do their best to maintain friendly relationships with their clients' lawyers. Still, a new attorney may swim into the pool; there are always hordes of ambitious lawyers swarming around, eager to latch on to potential clients. Your clients may be exposed to one of them during the course of the mediation. For example, one woman was persuaded to sue the mediator after her divorce lawyer forced her former husband to increase alimony. The court dismissed her claim because she could not prove that her husband would have offered more money in the original mediation.

Lawsuits against mediators are exceedingly rare and seldom successful. Nevertheless, some family mediators have taken out malpractice insurance of the kind sponsored by the Academy of Family Mediators. A few state laws provide immunity for mediators, but in any case you should have a provision in your retainer agreement protecting you, as a neutral party, against liability (intentional harm, however, is grounds for a suit even so). That provision should be carefully explained to the clients. A similar waiver should be incorporated in the final settlement.

Mediators may also be subject to complaints filed with their professional associations. According to its president, Robert Benjamin, the Academy of Family Mediators, which has almost 3,500 members, receives several such complaints each year (Benjamin, 1996). The academy provides a grievance procedure for such complaints. If the person complained against is an academy member and the complaint arises out of mediation services, it will be reviewed by the ethics committee to determine whether the complaint involves a violation of the Standards of Practice, leading to the appointment of a reviewing panel or the issuance of a reprimand. If a reviewing panel is appointed, further fact-finding takes place. The panel may issue a reprimand, suspend the respondent's membership, order restitution, or dismiss the complaint (Academy of Family Mediators, Policies and Procedures for Processing Complaints Against Members, 1992).

Lawyer mediators may also be subject to grievances filed with state or local bar associations; other mediators may have similar complaints filed with their primary professional organizations.

Mediators serving in court-administered or community-based programs may be monitored by a variety of organizational mechanisms. In coming years such supervision may become more onerous, particularly if states pass licensing regulations.

Other Sources of Work: Nondivorce Cases

In addition to divorce cases, other kinds of family disputes can be mediated.

Premarital Agreements

Couples frequently live together without being married. Some of them eventually marry, which can create significant changes in their legal relationship. Premarital negotiations and planning are increasingly common, especially among wealthy couples, for whom issues of ownership or substantial legal liability may be considerable. By negotiating a premarital agreement, the parties can protect their respective interests; the interests of children from a prior marriage or relationship may also be involved. A mediator with expertise in financial planning or tax problems may be particularly helpful in negotiating such agreements.

Approximately 3.6 million unmarried couples were living together in the United States in 1994 (*Information Please Almanac*, 1996, p. 836). In such households, even where there are no children, disagreements may arise over splitting the bills, paying the rent or mortgage, and the like. If they break up, couples may quarrel over the allocation of property or which of them can stay in the apartment. These disputes are much like those of a married couple, and they can be mediated in the same way.

Community mediation centers often take on such cases. Here is an example: Marla had recently moved to the area. She shared an apartment with Joe. They slept together, but Joe dated other women. One night he came home drunk; Marla heard him stumbling up the stairs and locked him out of the apartment, but he broke open the door. When she tried to call the police, he threw the telephone at her face and Marla ended up at the hospital bleeding. After several days, she went home to her family.

When Marla returned, she filed a criminal complaint and the court referred the case to mediation. To the mediator, Joe admitted he had been drinking that night but claimed Marla had no right to keep him out of the apartment. He said the telephone had slipped out of his hand; he loved Marla and had not meant to hurt her. But Marla felt differently, saying that Joe often became violent when he drank. There had been other incidents, and now she was afraid to live with him.

The community mediator asked Marla whether she would drop the charges if Joe would move out of the apartment and pay her hospital bill. She agreed. The deal was that Joe would continue to pay half the rent until the lease ran out in two months, and then the apartment would be in Marla's name. According to the community mediator, this resolved the problem admirably. The couple had fallen into a bad lifestyle; Marla only wanted to get out of it, so there was no need for a criminal trial. It is typical in community mediation to convert a potential criminal case into a behavioral dispute that can then be resolved through negotiations.

Homosexual Partners

Mediation often is the best way to settle disputes between homosexual couples. According to Douglas M. McIntyre's 1994 article "Gay Parents," "research demonstrates that gay men and lesbian women are systematically discriminated against by the legal system" (McIntyre, 1994, p. 136). A judge may regard homosexuality as deviant, but a mediator can be selected who holds no such view.

One such case involved a valuable art collection that had been assembled by two men during the many years they had lived together. Their relationship was such that no records had been kept of who paid for which paintings. When they finally split up, they were unable to allocate the art. A mutually selected mediator helped them to design a blind auction, which resolved the problem.

Teenagers and Their Parents

Some people find it difficult to remain objective when the authority of a parent is being challenged by an adolescent. One family court judge complained about an incident in her court this way: "I could not believe what I was hearing. When I was a girl, we were never permitted to question our parents. Here I was, listening to that little brat calling her father a fool, calling him names in front of her mother and her little brother. I could hardly keep my temper."

As adolescent children become more assertive, quarrels break out with their parents over all kinds of issues. Disputes about the use of a family automobile, educational expenses, or sharing household work can be troublesome. Other controversies may include staying out of school, using drugs, or running away. The parents can have such a child placed under family court supervision, but it may be more appropriate to settle such disputes privately, perhaps with the help of a mediator.

Children who are taken to court for serious offenses are called "status offenders." The court can remove them from the home for placement in an institution or, after a hearing, place them on probation. That may not cure the underlying problem, which may be caused by the emotional climate within the family. When a child has broken the law, the case may have to be resolved in court, but perhaps through a court mediation program. Courts may not have enough time to devote to what is essentially a dispute between children and their parents. A private resolution might be more appropriate.

The role of adolescent children has changed with the times. Among immigrant families, children sometimes serve as a bridge between adult members of the family and the community; they translate community standards for their parents. In a rapidly changing society, many young people help their parents cope with wrenching readjustments. In earlier days, the village elders were the mediators. Now, children may have to teach their elders about the popular culture and the computerized world.

A family does not have to be poor to encounter behavioral problems with adolescents. With the assistance of a private mediator, parents can reach an understanding between themselves on what to do about their child's behavior. If one wants to discipline the child and the other does not, the rift may encourage the child to indulge in even worse behavior, as well as sour the relationship between the parents.

These kinds of problems can be negotiated. The parents can propose guidelines describing the kind of behavior they will allow and then reach an agreement on it with the child. By exchanging promises, an acceptable regime for the future can be entered into. Once accepted by the child, the parents must abide by and enforce the contract; love and discipline are closely related.

Rather than trying to solve some problems with a child, some parents give up and in extreme cases even turn the child out of the house. This rarely solves a child's behavioral problems. To be made homeless is to suffer the most extreme punishment that parents can impose; in most cases it would be far better to attempt resolution through negotiations. Mediation encourages face-to-face discussions so that a certain amount of behavioral modification can take place.

Community mediation centers encounter children who have run away from home because they are afraid of being punished for breaking parental rules. The relationship between the parents' inability to communicate and the imposition of harsh discipline may be obvious. Mediators can help a family resolve disciplinary problems without resorting to corporal punishment.

There are no easy answers to adolescent behavioral problems. Every family has to find its own way through those troubled years, but an outside mediator can provide helpful guidance based on experience with similar cases. It is a good sign when parents learn to resolve such disputes without anger. Laughter and love don't hurt either.

Schools and Parents

Every public school student has the right to receive appropriate educational services. For students who qualify, special services must be provided by the school district. Those kinds of services are expensive, so disputes often occur between parents and school authorities.

Parents may claim that their child is learning disabled and eligible to receive special services. If the school rejects the claim, various legal reviews are available, but mediation may be a better way to resolve the dispute. A mediator can meet with parents and school authorities independently, then bring them together to explore the alternatives. Perhaps a less expensive program is available and acceptable to the parents. A mediator can explore the options, explain them to the parents, and sometimes obtain concessions from the school authorities. The flexibility of mediation can serve the interests of all.

Teenage Pregnancy

When an unmarried teenager becomes pregnant, disputes between the prospective mother and father, and sometimes the parents of either or both, are common. Is marriage a possibility? If not, who is going to take responsibility for the child? Are abortion or adoption to be considered? All these questions involve the rights and responsibilities of various people, including the father. Such matters are highly emotional, involving issues of morality and public policy, but are often decided privately, without court intervention.

If the mother decides to keep and raise her baby herself, arrangements have to be made for its support. Sometimes the father may agree to bear part of the burden, as may his or the mother's parents; or any or all may refuse. The mother also may qualify for public assistance. Who must pay for support and at what levels is often negotiated privately, in which case a mediator may help decide in a less emotional atmosphere than might otherwise prevail.

Other Family Disputes

As most of us have experienced, there are many other areas of disagreement within families. Usually problems can be worked out by those involved, but sometimes mediation is the best road to resolution. Here are some examples.

Relocation. Disagreements may arise when a spouse receives a promotion or job offer that requires moving elsewhere. In one case, a rising male executive received a promotion that required relocating from the East Coast to Kansas, and the other members of the family were unhappy. One son had just started a business. Another would have to leave his friends at the local high school. The daughter, still living at home, had recently taken a job in New York. After listening to the children's complaints, the executive's wife refused to move unless everyone was satisfied. For several months the father lived in a hotel room in Kansas, flying home every weekend to discuss the problem. For a time, it seemed likely that he and his wife would separate, but an agreement was worked out when a family friend volunteered to act as mediator. The father agreed to purchase an apartment for the two older children and pay private school tuition for the younger son. On that basis, his wife joined him in Kansas.

Nursing Care. When a family member retires, sometimes other family members have to adjust their lifestyles. When an elderly member of the family requires nursing care and did not (or could not) make arrangements to pay for it, family arrangements have to be made. The necessary trade-offs may be best handled with the help of a mediator.

Family Businesses. Control of family-owned companies can become an issue, especially after a founder or subsequent owner dies. How should income from the business be allocated, and who should run it? Rather than answering such questions in court, where the company will be subjected to legal expenses, a judicial decision, and public disclosure, private mediation can help. A mediator can be selected who has extensive business experience as well as sensitivity to the personal relationships between family members. Many family businesses have been harmed by protracted lawsuits over matters that could have been settled in mediation.

Some closely held corporations place dispute resolution provisions in their bylaws so that disagreements between the investors can be resolved privately. There has been a trend in recent years to use such systems to resolve all kinds of business disputes. The alternative dispute resolution (ADR) movement is motivated by the desire of business executives to keep their companies out of court, anticipating that they will save money by turning to ADR.

Inheritance. Differences over the meaning and application of wills and trust agreements sometimes result in bitter family controversies, creating lifetime feuds between the contestants. In attempting to referee such disputes, the family's regular lawyer may become a pariah with one branch of the family. Mediation may eliminate the need for that attorney to take sides; through it the relatives can work out their own solutions. The mediator in such a case should probably be another attorney who is familiar with the applicable legal and tax considerations but is demonstrably impartial to all concerned.

Violence. When disagreements in a family escalate into violence, the use of alcohol or other drugs may be involved. Many such confrontations can be avoided if the family learns how to resolve disagreements peacefully through negotiation.

Loss of jobs, illness, and reduced social services can combine to increase the stress on many families; sometimes violence results. Unless criminal court involvement becomes appropriate, disputants may be able to solve their problems through mediation when they otherwise could never reconcile; mediation not only resolves disagreements, but teaches participants how to avoid physical confrontations in the future by collaborating or bargaining.

How to Market Mediation Services

Like any service offered to the public, family mediation must be marketed. To become established in the field, you will have to develop a strategy to gain customers, and you may rely at the outset on referrals. Some mediators receive referrals from attorneys. Lawyers who do not handle divorce cases may routinely send couples to family mediation; others may work out property issues in a marital separation but refer clients to a mediator trained in family therapy to discuss child custody.

Clients are also referred by other professionals or by friends of the prospective clients. You need to be known as a competent family mediator throughout your community, particularly among professionals who come in contact with divorcing couples or others with difficult family conflicts. Such contacts might include staff members of social agencies, religious organizations, and hospitals as well as others involved in family counseling.

It is inappropriate for a family mediator to pay commissions, rebates, or similar forms of remuneration to people for such referrals. That does not mean you cannot be friends with them or even do favors for them. They are a source of business for your services; somehow they must become aware of your interest.

Joyce Hauser's *Good Divorces, Bad Divorces* (1995) contains useful information on how to publicize your services. She suggests marketing plans that target the consumer as well as the legal and mental health professions and recommends promotions via television and radio, particularly talk shows (she hosted one in New York City). Hauser suggests that mediators start campaigns, preferably with a dramatic title such as "There Is Such a Thing as a Good Divorce," and recommends that public relations be supplemented by promotional booklets. Her book contains sample scripts, print advertisements, and a draft for an eight-page promotional booklet, plus a model press kit with recommendations as to how it should be used. She says a mediator's press kit should include a résumé demonstrating credentials as well as a glossy photograph.

Hauser also recommends that family mediators give talks to community organizations on such topics as "A New Life After Divorce" and "Making Peace with the Past." She suggests talking about successful divorce rather than blatantly advertising mediation services.

Another way to present yourself to the community is to sponsor seminars on divorce or family mediation. You can invite prominent experts to participate with you on a panel drawn from the community you serve or intend to serve. In addition to displaying your wares, such seminars make it possible for you to educate the community about the benefits of mediation. Training programs can also be a source of income. Some of the best-known family mediators have developed training as a business, providing seminars on their own and offering their services for a fee to other trainers. That way, they acquire a reputation and generate income.

Joyce Hauser notes that surveys can draw attention and create interest in family mediation, especially if press releases about them start out with something like: "A new study shows . . ."

Publicizing family mediation requires imagination, hard work, and some knowledge of public relations. But whatever you do is likely to gain visibility both for yourself and for the service you are trying to market.

Some mediators practice with family mediation centers, which you will find listed in the phone book under "mediation." Don't assume the practitioners listed there are all family mediators. Some may specialize in insurance claims, construction or labor cases, or other specialties unrelated to family mediation.

The Academy of Family Mediators provides a free referral service that can put you in touch with family mediators in your area, as well as regional mediation groups and training centers; the phone number is (617) 674–2663.

A mediation practice may be broader than family mediation. There are other centers of activity, including the community mediation centers mentioned several times before. These are often partially financed by the state court system; they provide an alternative to litigation. Cases may be referred by police precincts or criminal court administrators. With the help of a mediator, the charging party and the accused party attempt to negotiate a resolution of their dispute. The clients usually come from disadvantaged neighborhoods; the cases often involve family disputes and disagreements between unmarried people who are living together. By volunteering to serve as a mediator in such a program, you may be able to obtain useful training and practice in mediation.

Another form of institutionalized mediation involves employment disputes. Many employers have established internal mediation programs or ombudsmen to assist employees with their personal disputes, usually as part of an employee assistance program; they may use outside mediators. Some also use mediation to resolve discrimination claims or contested firings. Mediators who handle employment cases are not necessarily family mediators, but some cross the line.

In addition to these areas of practice, a rapidly increasing number of business claims are being mediated. Among them are personal injury and property damage claims against insurance companies and self-insureds, disputes over construction projects, claims against stockbrokers, and disagreements over real estate. Mediation is now a compulsory part of some civil court systems, where parties are required to mediate before being given an opportunity to try their case before a judge or jury. The use of mediation has expanded in recent years because people recognize the importance of resolving disputes out of court, which is what this book is all about.

Summary

Becoming a family mediator is a matter of inclination, skill, and education. At present the profession is largely unregulated, so a private family mediator does not have to be an attorney or any other type of professional. Still, all family mediators must observe certain ethical and legal constraints, and must know the basics of domestic relations law and other pertinent laws even though they must refrain from giving direct legal advice to clients. Training, especially as offered or recommended by the Academy of Family Mediators, is advised. To gain clients for family mediation, marketing and networking may be necessary, and exploring all market niches is best.

Family mediation allows family members to resolve their disputes through bargaining and collaboration. I wrote this book to explain how the process works. If you decide to become a family mediator after reading it, I'm delighted. If you have only learned to think like a family mediator, I'm equally gratified.

References

Academy of Family Mediators. *Policies and Procedures for Processing Complaints Against Members*. Academy of Family Mediators, 1992.

Academy of Family Mediators. *Standards of Practice for Family and Divorce Mediation*. Academy of Family Mediators, 1995.

Ahrons, C. *The Good Divorce*. New York: HarperCollins, 1994.

Benjamin, R. D. "Ethical and Professional Predicaments: Complaints Against Mediators: Some Practical Hints." AFM *Mediation News*, 1996, *14*(4), 5.

Bush, R. B. "The Dilemmas of Mediation Practice: A Study of Ethical Dilemmas and Policy Implications." Unpublished report to the National Institute of Dispute Resolution, 1992.

Coogler, O. J. *Structured Mediation in Divorce Settlements: A Handbook for Marital Mediators*. Lexington, Mass.: Heath, 1978.

"The Family." *The Economist*, Sept. 9, 1995, pp. 25–27.

Gaschen, D. A. "Mandatory Custody Mediation: The Debate Over Its Usefulness Continues." *Ohio State Journal on Dispute Resolution*, 1995, *10*(2), 469–490.

Grebe, S. C. "Building on Structured Mediation: An Integrated Model for Mediation of Separation and Divorce." *Mediation Quarterly*, 1994, *12*(1), 15–35.

Grillo, T. "The Mediation Process: Dangers for Women." *100 Yale Law Journal*, 1991, 1,545.

Harrell, S. J. "Why Attorneys Attend Mediation Sessions." *Mediation Quarterly*, 1995, *12*(4), 369–377.

Hauser, J. *Good Divorces, Bad Divorces*. Lanham: University Press of America, 1995.

Haynes, J. M. *Mediating Divorce: Casebook of Strategies for Successful Family Negotiations*. San Francisco: Jossey-Bass, 1984.

Hoffman, J. "Divorce Lawyers Fear They Protested Too Much." *The New York Times*, Jan. 1, 1996, pp. 33 and 36.

Information Please Almanac. Boston: Houghton Mifflin, 1996.

Kelly, J. "Developing and Implementing Post-Divorce Parenting Plans." In *Non-Residential Parenting: New Vistas in Family Living*. Newbury Park, Calif.: Sage, 1993.

McIntyre, D. H. "Gay Parents and Child Custody." *Mediation Quarterly*, 1994, *12*(2), 135–149.

Milne, A. "Custody of Children in a Divorce Process: A Family Self-Determination Model." *Conciliation Courts Review*, 1978, *16*(2), 1–10.

"Obituary of Lee Marvin." *The New York Times*, Aug. 17, 1987, p. 17.

Pearson, J., and Thoennes, N. "Divorce Mediation: Reflections on a Decade of Research." In Kressel, and others (eds.), *Mediation Research: The Process and Effectiveness of Third-Party Intervention*. San Francisco: Jossey-Bass, 1989, pp. 15–18.

Ricci, I. M. *Mom's House, Dad's House: Making Shared Custody Work*. New York: Macmillan, 1980.

Taylor, A. "The Four Foundations of Family Mediation Training: Implications for Training and Certification." *Mediation Quarterly*, 1994, *12*(1), 77–89.

Tidwell, A. C. "Not Effective Communication but Effective Persuasion." *Mediation Quarterly*, 1994, *12*(1), 3–14.

United Nations. *Demographic Yearbook*. New York: United Nations, 1992.

Wallerstein, J. S., and Kelly, J. B. *Surviving the Breakup: How Children and Parents Cope with Divorce*. New York: Basic Books, 1980.

Index